CONSTRUCTION CRAFT SUPERVISION

Michael Hatchett

B T BATSFORD LIMITED · LONDON

in association with the Chartered Institute of Building

First published 1992

Typeset by Deltatype Ltd, Ellesmere Port, Cheshire
Printed and bound in Great Britain by
Dotesios Ltd, Trowbridge, Wiltshire.

Published by B T Batsford Ltd
4 Fitzhardinge Street, London W1H 0AH

A catalogue record for this book is
available from the British Library

ISBN 0 7134 6402 X

ACKNOWLEDGMENT

The stimulus for my involvement in supervisory development and training within the construction industry came originally from Mr D. A. G. Reid and Mr A. O. Williams of the Brixton School of Building and from Professor K. E. Thurley of the London School of Economics in the mid 1960s, without whose early help and guidance this book would never have been possible. During the last 30 years I have received immense support for my work from many sources, in particular from the staff and members of the Building Employers Confederation, the Chartered Institute of Building, the Construction Industry Training Board and the staff and my fellow examiners of the City and Guilds of London Institute, none of whom are responsible for any faults and shortcomings which appear in this book. I also acknowledge the considerable help given by many first line supervisors in testing some of the ideas contained in it. I therefore hope that I have, in some small way, repaid the massive debt that I owe to all those who have helped me during my work with first line supervisors, by passing on my collective experiences for the benefit of others.

Amersham 1992   M. H.

CONTENTS

INTRODUCTION

The principles of construction craft supervision are the concern of this book. The term **craft supervision** has been used to cover a range of occupational titles related to the first level of supervision in the construction industry including, charge-hand, trade foreman, craft foreman, ganger and supervisor.

Essentially, first line supervisors are located at the workplace and are directly responsible for construction work. They may be site or workshop based and may be employed by general contractors, specialist contractors, manufacturers or direct service organizations. Wherever they are employed, first line supervisors are an essential and crucial link in the management of the construction process. In addition they form one of the most highly populated categories of supervisory occupations within the industry.

Almost without exception first line supervisors are recruited from the ranks of the operatives they will be supervising, and traditionally the majority of first line supervisors have received little or no specialized supervisory training either before or during their careers as supervisors. In recent years greater emphasis has been placed on supervisory training by the Construction Industry Training Board, the Building Employers Confederation and the Chartered Institute of Building.

This text, therefore, addresses the main principles of construction craft supervision and has been written specifically for first line supervisors, for those responsible for training first line supervisors, and for those concerned with the structure and management of organizations in which first line construction supervisors are employed. It is intended as a basic guide for first line supervisors, as a companion text for those preparing for the City and Guilds of London Institute examination in Craft Supervision within the 600 series of Construction Crafts Supplementary Studies, and as a supporting text for first line supervisory training courses associated with the construction industry. The book has been structured so that the early chapters address general issues and the later chapters more specific supervisory issues. It is anticipated that those with personal knowledge of supervision within the construction industry will supplement these principles of craft supervision with their own practical experience. For those wishing to examine topics in greater depth, references to other texts are given at the end of each chapter.

CHAPTER ONE

THE INDUSTRIAL FRAMEWORK

This chapter establishes the framework of the UK construction industry within which craft supervisors operate. It describes an industry which is fragmented and labour intensive, and it highlights a number of settings in which craft supervisors are employed.

THE UK CONSTRUCTION INDUSTRY

The UK construction industry is large, fragmented and organizationally complex. The term **construction** includes civil engineering, building, specialist building, and a range of associated mechanical and electrical services. The construction industry normally employs rather more than one million people in construction operations, and rather less than another million in the associated professions, and in the manufacture and supply of materials and components to the industry.

THE SIZE OF FIRMS IN THE CONSTRUCTION INDUSTRY

The industry contains some 100,000 construction firms of which about 90% employ less than 25 people. It is therefore mainly an industry of small firms. However, there are a few very large construction organizations each of which directly employ rather more than a thousand people, and who together are responsible for some 25% of all the work completed by the whole industry.

THE WORKLOAD OF THE CONSTRUCTION INDUSTRY

The workload of the industry, which can exceed some £20 billion each year, but which can also fluctuate widely depending upon the general state of the economy, is divided into new construction, and work to existing buildings. Work to existing buildings in the UK has tended to increase in percentage terms in recent years so that it now almost equals the value of new construction work completed each year.

New construction has traditionally been divided into work for the public sector and work for the private sector; and into:

INDUSTRIAL SECTORS	• housing – which can be either in the private or the public sector

- public works – such as hospitals and roads
- commercial and industrial projects.

Work to existing buildings may be divided into:

WORK TO EXISTING BUILDINGS	
	• maintenance and repair
	• conservation
	• improvements
	• adaptations, and
	• extensions.

SPECIALIZATION

Few organizations associated with construction are involved across the whole range of available work, and most specialize to some extent. Some specialize in working for either the public or the private sector, some in either new construction or maintenance, some concentrate on larger or smaller projects and some specialize in particular construction operations or services.

The workload and the structure of the industry are not, however, static but change over time; sometimes these changes are turbulent and extensive and at others slow and limited in extent. Craft supervisors operate within this complex and changing industrial framework.

CRAFT SUPERVISION: THE FIRST LINE OF MANAGEMENT

Craft supervision may be defined as that level of supervision or management that is workplace based, and which is directly responsible for construction work. It is therefore the first line of management in the construction industry.

The term **craft supervision** is used to cover a range of occupational titles, including charge-hand, trade foreman, craft foreman, ganger, and supervisor, and is not restricted to the traditional building crafts. Any person with such a title is therefore directly responsible for the work of others, and is expected to have some personal knowledge, skill and experience of the work being supervised.

SHOULD A CRAFT SUPERVISOR WORK OR SUPERVISE?

It has been the custom for **craft** supervisors in the construction industry to be appointed from the occupations contributing to the work being supervised. The previous work experience of craft supervisors often leads to uncertainty regarding the extent to which a supervisor should be expected to participate in the work of the team, and there are a number of factors which might influence such a decision. These include:

TO WORK OR TO SUPERVISE DEPENDS UPON	• the complexity of the work being supervised • the geographical area over which the team is spread • the number of people in the team • the other duties allocated to the supervisor.

As a very rough guide, a supervisor could be allocated one hour of supervisory time with each team member. Therefore, with a team of four, a supervisor could reasonably be expected to spend half the day in supervisory activities and half the day working with the team. With a team of eight, it would be reasonable for a craft supervisor to be fully involved in supervisory activities, and with a team of more than eight the supervisory functions might need to be shared between two or more supervisors. Where the work is technically complex, dispersed over a wide area, or where the supervisor has other duties and responsibilities, the team will often contain less than eight operatives.

THE CRAFT SUPERVISOR AS PART OF THE MANAGEMENT STRUCTURE

It is vital that, regardless of how few people there are in the team being supervised, or of how much time the supervisor spends on manual work with the team, the craft supervisor is both recognized and accepted as being part of the management structure of the organization. It is completely inappropriate for the craft supervisor to be treated as a manual worker one day and a supervisor the next.

To be effective the craft supervisor should at all times behave as part of the management team, and when engaged in manual work should be setting the rest of the team a good example of what management expects of an employee. This can, of course, place the craft supervisor in a very difficult position, because the supervisor may not be the most skilled, the most experienced, or even the fastest worker in the team, and for this reason many craft supervisors dislike participating in manual work once they have been appointed to a supervisory position.

THE CRAFT SUPERVISOR AS 'THE MAN IN THE MIDDLE'

This image of the craft supervisor as part of the management team sometimes presents difficulties. In many organizations management has the status associated with head office, a company car and a monthly salary. In contrast, the craft supervisor is usually site based, has few company perks and will probably have an hourly or weekly wage. As a result the craft supervisor can all too easily be found in the middle ground between workers and managers, and in extreme cases accepted and trusted by neither.

This situation should be strenuously avoided. Employers should consider carefully how much status should be given to an individual supervisor upon appointment, and supervisors should consider how they are going to earn the respect and trust of both their teams and their senior management.

Against this general background a number of different settings for craft supervision will now be considered.

CRAFT SUPERVISION WITHIN GENERAL CONTRACTING

A general contractor may be defined as a private sector firm with an overall contractual responsibility for construction contracts. The main, or general, contractor came into existence in Britain during the first half of the nineteenth century and has become, until recently, the principal method of organizing work within the private sector of the construction industry.

Usually, the main contractor directly employs people in many of the frequently occurring occupations required on a range of construction projects, and supplements these employees, as necessary, with sub-contractors appointed for specialist work on individual projects.

In recent years the amount of work sub-contracted has tended to increase. Many main contractors have, as a result, increased their management activities, and correspondingly decreased their direct involvement in craft supervision, which has therefore become the responsibility of sub-contractors.

Traditionally, many main contractors sought to give continuity of employment by limiting the range of occupations they would directly employ, and by seeking a succession of projects requiring broadly similar types of work over long periods of time. Around this strategy developed a career progression, starting with craft apprenticeship and progressing through the craft occupations, craft and general foremanship and contracts management, to the senior management of the firm. Thus, those employed as craft supervisors within such firms could often look back to their days as an apprentice and forward to their future as general foreman, agent, or senior manager with the same employer.

This type of firm, with its long term direct employment and internal career development strategies, is generally considered to be almost suited to relatively stable business conditions, and often finds it more difficult to cope with industrial turbulence and relatively uncertain economic and social conditions. There are, however, many general contractors still in existence who are continuing to provide long term employment and career progression opportunities for craft supervisors.

CRAFT SUPERVISION WITHIN SINGLE TRADE CONTRACTING

A single trade contractor is one which, as the name suggests, undertakes construction work within a limited occupational or skill range. Single trade contractors originated with the mediaeval craft guilds, survived through the general contracting era as specialist sub-contractors and have recently come back into greater prominence as a consequence of the development of new forms of procurement, including management contracting.

Many single trade contractors have tended to place an emphasis on craft technology and practice and, as a consequence, have a relatively simple organizational structure with few levels of management. Thus the craft supervisor in a single trade firm can have a higher status than a counterpart within a general contractor. Of course, many single trade firms are relatively small in size, compared with large general contractors, and consequently need fewer people in management positions. This is not always the case, however, and frequently a single trade sub-contractor may find that the party with whom they have a contract is smaller and less experienced in construction work than they are.

The craft supervisor within a single trade firm may already possess considerable trade experience, not necessarily based on an apprenticeship, and may look forward to a position as contracts supervisor or contracts manager. Within many of the larger single trade firms there are also opportunities for craft supervisors to move to more technical occupations, particularly as estimators or surveyors.

However, there is less opportunity for progression within the smaller single trade firms, and some craft supervisors branch out and form their own businesses. With many site-based construction occupations the limited capital required to start a new business makes the step from craft supervisor to small scale employer a relatively easy one to take. Of course, it is one thing to set up a new business and quite another to make that business successful.

Being a competent supervisor is not the only skill required to run a successful business. As a consequence, some supervisors will move from employee to employer status, and back again, several times during their working lives within the construction industry.

CRAFT SUPERVISION WITHIN A WORKSHOP ENVIRONMENT

There are some construction trades which are not just site based and which do not move from site to site as work progresses, but have their own off-site workshops making components for site assembly and fixing. Some of the most common examples are those associated with joinery, plastering, stonemasonry and metalwork fabrication.

In such firms there are often two different types of craft supervisor: those responsible for the workshop-based manufacture and fabrication of components, and those responsible for their site assembly and fixing. This division of some construction crafts into separate elements of making and fixing has brought its own complexities and supervisory skills.

Some of the principal site-based complexities are associated with:

SITE ASSEMBLY AND FIXING INVOLVES	<ul><li>obtaining site dimensions</li><li>determining appropriate manufacturing tolerances</li><li>communicating site information to the workshop-based team</li><li>moving prefabricated components into position on site</li><li>establishing appropriate methods of fixing</li><li>protecting finished work from damage by other trades.</li></ul>

In addition, the shop supervisor often has to ensure that machines and operatives are kept fully, economically and safely occupied, whilst producing several independent flows of components to meet the various production needs of different projects.

In the larger workshops the shop supervisor will often be part of a team including drawing office staff, setting-out specialists, estimators and buyers, whereas in the smaller workshops the supervisor may be personally responsible for most of the day to day production activities.

In either case, the shop supervisor and the site supervisors must collaborate effectively, and thus need to build up effective working relationships over a range of projects and types of work.

CRAFT SUPERVISION WITHIN DIRECT SERVICE ORGANIZATIONS

In direct service, or direct labour, organizations the client, or building owner, directly employs the people doing the construction work. Traditionally, the term is used in connection with public sector organizations, such as local authorities, although there are many private sector building owners who directly employ their own construction operatives and their own supervisory, managerial and technical support staff. There are both advantages and disadvantages to using direct labour for construction work.

Many public sector direct service organizations have attempted to be model employers, applying to the letter central government recommendations and nationally negotiated agreements on issues such as equal employment opportunities, training, safety, health and welfare. This **model employer** approach has resulted in organizations which have tended to become, over many years, less competitive than their private sector counterparts. The managers of direct service organizations also often find it rather more difficult to restructure quickly without incurring industrial relations difficulties, because of their historical relationships with trade unions and their support for joint industrial negotiations.

As a consequence, public sector direct service organizations have tended to be:

THE STRENGTHS OF DIRECT SERVICE ORGANIZA- TIONS	• strong supporters of apprenticeship and other nationally recognized vocational training schemes • more interested in providing secure conditions of employment • more committed to promoting from within the organization

and therefore tend to have rather more stable and long serving work forces than is the case within the private sector of the industry.

Many direct service organizations have tended to specialize in repairs and maintenance, and have therefore developed specialist work teams and supervisory skills in such work.

SUMMARY

Thus it is possible to identify at least four very different organizational environments within which craft supervisors might be employed:

- general contracting
- single trade firms
- craft workshops
- direct service organization.

Each has its own industrial characteristics, its own strengths and weaknesses, and its own framework of customs and practices within which craft supervisors operate.

FURTHER STUDY OPPORTUNITIES

The following cover the industrial framework of the construction industry in more detail:

BOWLEY, M. E. A., *The British Building Industry: four studies in response and resistance to change*, Cambridge University Press 1966

COLCLOUGH, J. R., *The Construction Industry of Great Britain*, Butterworth 1965

GRAY, C. and FLANAGAN, R., *The Changing Role of Specialist and Trade Contractors*, Chartered Institute of Building 1989

HARPER, D. *et al*, *1980–90 The Future of Building and its National Federation*, A report to the NFBTE 1979

MORRIS, K., *Small Building Firms – their Origins, Characteristics and Development Needs*, Occasional Paper no 32, Chartered Institute of Building nd

POWELL, C. G., *An Economic History of the British Building Industry 1815–1979*, The Architectural Press 1980

POSTGATE, R. W., *The Builders' History*, London, The National Federation of Building Trade Operatives 1923

TRESSELL, R., *The Ragged Trousered Philanthropists*, Granada 1965 and reprinted many times

CHAPTER TWO

THE ORGANIZATIONAL FRAMEWORK

This chapter considers some organizational matters which are relevant to craft supervision. It describes some of the basic characteristics of organizational structure, the function of job guides and some of the factors which should be examined when establishing and developing effective operating procedures for craft supervisors. Some of the basic requirements of record systems are explored and examples are given to illustrate some of the issues that arise in everyday craft supervision.

ORGANIZATIONAL STRUCTURE – A DEFINITION

Organizational structure may be defined as the network of formally stated and reasonably durable relationships and arrangements found inside organizations.

THE FUNCTIONS OF ORGANIZATIONAL STRUCTURE

Organizational structure attempts to perform three major functions. First, it provides opportunities for organizations to reduce external and internal uncertainty. The activities of **forecasting**, **research** and **planning** can help to reduce external uncertainty, and those associated with **quality**, **cost** and **production** are designed to reduce uncertainty arising from variable behaviour within the organization. Secondly, it seeks to assist an organization to undertake a wide variety of activities through strategies associated with **departmentalization**, **specialization**, **division of labour** and **delegation of authority**. Finally, it helps an organization to keep its activities **co-ordinated** and **in focus**. Formal committees and information systems are aspects of structure that are designed to assist in integrating organizational activities.

There are two principal features of organizational structure; the easily visible departmental structure and the less visible organizational culture, authority relationships, attitudes, specializations and networks of controls.

DEPARTMENTAL STRUCTURE

There are three principal forms of organizational departmentalization, the functional form, the divisional form and the matrix structure.

The functional form

The functional form of organizational structure is used where all those people who can contribute to the fulfilment of a particular function are grouped together. Thus surveyors are grouped separately from estimators. Co-ordination between functional departments can be a problem because each separate group tends to develop its own goals and preferred ways of working.

The divisional form

In the divisional form all those functions associated with a particular project are grouped together. There can be different types of divisional structure; by product – such as housing or civil engineering, by territory or even by customer. An organization may be divisionalized at one level and functionally structured at another level. The divisional form is also not without problems because there is a tendency for each division to have its own support services, computer facilities, and offices which may not be economically used within a single division.

The matrix form

A third principle of structural grouping is the matrix organization. Typically each member of a matrix organization is a member of two groups, one of which is more or less permanent and the other more or less temporary. For example, a builder's surveyor may be permanently located in the surveying department but assigned to one or more specific projects. On completion of these projects the surveyor would revert back to the central surveying department until assigned other sites or projects. Thus the matrix organization is a combination of the principle of specialized departments with the principle of more or less autonomous units. It is used mainly in situations where a number of temporary projects are common. Some individuals do not find it easy to work within matrix organizations because they usually have to adjust their own, or their department's, preferred working methods to meet the specific requirements of each temporary unit.

DEPARTMENTAL CULTURE

The less visible aspects of organizational structure are associated with the deep set beliefs about the way in which work should be organized, the way authority should be exercised, and people rewarded and controlled. Four principal organizational cultures have been recognized. These are:

ORGANIZA-TION CULTURES	• **power cultures**, which are highly political forms of organization in which control is maintained principally through the selection of individuals for key positions within the organization

- **role cultures** which offer security and predictability to individuals and which tend to be more effective in stable business environments
- **task cultures** in which the emphasis is placed upon getting the job done, and in which greater emphasis can often be placed upon the ends rather than the means of completing the task
- **person cultures** in which the individual is the central point and in which organizational structure is minimal.

These cultures are seldom obvious to the casual observer or to the newly appointed supervisor and often only become apparent through careful observation. Bringing about radical changes in the culture of an organization through the deliberate actions of senior management can be both difficult to achieve successfully and traumatic for the participants.

POLICY ISSUES

The craft supervisor occupies a key position in any organization, operating from a position where the plans and policies of senior management are turned into practical actions by operatives. In large organizations with very formal structures, it is normal for policy issues to be negotiated and formally stated in company handbooks. There are often internal procedures for reviewing and for consulting with staff about changes in policy, and for ensuring that all employees are kept informed of the changes in organizational policy which touch and concern their work.

In smaller, less formal organizations, or where more autocratic styles of management operate, policy issues are seldom written down or negotiated, and are mostly established through performance. In such situations, first line supervisors develop a knowledge and an understanding of policy issues through:

UNDER-STANDING POLICY ISSUES THROUGH . . .	<ul><li>planned work experience</li><li>careful observation of the performance of other people within the organization</li><li>questioning their line managers about areas of uncertainty</li><li>trial and error.</li></ul>

COMMON POLICY ISSUES

There is no finite set of policy issues which are relevant to first line supervision, but there are a number of matters which arise sufficiently regularly for them to be matters of concern for most organizations. Sometimes they will be formally negotiated and communicated in writing, and sometimes they will simply become part of the customs and practices of the organization. However they are developed, most organizations will have some policies regarding:

COMMON POLICY ISSUES	• organizational structure and lines of communication • employment arrangements • customer relations • industrial relations • safety • materials procurement and usage • plant and equipment procurement and usage • productivity and quality • training.

Some of these matters, such as employment and safety, will be controlled to an extent by legislation. Others, such as industrial relations, may be largely the subject of national, industrial or local agreements with outside organizations. Yet others will be internal matters of policy of particular concern and interest to senior management as a whole, or to individual managers with special responsibilities for particular aspects of the work of the organization. Three of these issues will now be considered in greater detail.

EFFECTIVE LINES OF COMMUNICATION

Perhaps the most obvious starting point is to establish the position of the craft supervisor within the organizational structure, so that effective two-way lines of communication can be developed between operatives and management.

In all but the smallest organizations, management responsibilities are shared and there will be several people in more senior management positions than the craft supervisor. Difficulties soon emerge if several managers give conflicting instructions to the same supervisor, so it is normal for each craft supervisor to be linked with one specific manager who has an overall responsibility for the work of the craft supervisor and supporting team.

However, to funnel all communications through a single line management link is usually too restricting and many organizations encourage communication links between craft supervisors and other senior staff, such as plant or transport managers, safety officers, buyers, estimators or surveyors. The intention being to encourage the flow of information between members of the same organization without diluting specific line management responsibilities. These intentions are sometimes difficult to realize because of the personal strengths and weaknesses of individual line managers, and because of the speed with which organizations restructure in order to meet internal and external changes in demands.

CUSTOMER RELATIONS

Customer relations is a good example of a policy issue which might be viewed differently by managers with different special interests within the same organization.

Managers with responsibilities for publicity, marketing, sales and services will present an organization's policies regarding customer relations differently from those with responsibilities for production, programming, purchasing, safety and industrial relations. Also these specialist managers are likely to have a different view from those with line management responsibilities for cost recovery.

Similarly, long established or favoured customers, with whom special relationships have been built up over many years, may be treated differently from occasional or one-off customers. A craft supervisor may find, therefore, that policies regarding customer relations vary between departments and customers, and between and within projects. Also, as it is unlikely that these operating policies will be written down and clearly stated, they will probably be discovered as work proceeds.

MATERIALS, PLANT AND EQUIPMENT

The procurement and use of materials, plant and equipment can also raise important policy issues of concern to the craft supervisor.

With materials, policy decisions may be made about the degree of central or local purchasing to be used, about the sizes and methods of delivery and about appropriate allowances of waste. With plant and equipment there may be general policy issues about whether to hire or buy, and when hiring is considered appropriate, whether to hire from internal or external sources, with or without supporting design, installation, operating or maintenance services.

Sometimes first line supervisors will be involved in these decision-making processes, but at other times the decisions will have already been made and the supervisor is only required to implement effectively the consequences. Thus policy can be seen in some organizations as a mixture of long term stated intentions and short term operational strategies.

SUPERVISORY JOB GUIDES AND JOB DESCRIPTIONS

No two first line supervisors' jobs are exactly the same. There may be significant differences between and within employing organizations in terms of:

ORGANIZA- TIONAL DIF- FERENCES	• organizational structure • management attitudes and abilities • the skills, previous experience and attitudes of individual supervisors • the attitudes and abilities of their work teams • the technical requirements of specific projects.

Also, each of these elements of an individual supervisor's job might change in emphasis or content as a consequence of changes in personnel, operational procedures or the technical nature of the work. Many senior managers take the view that it is necessary to establish the main tasks and responsibilities within an organization without reference to the individuals who will be employed to undertake those tasks and responsibilities.

The following headings cover most of the key issues associated with a craft supervisory position:

CRAFT
SUPERVISION
THE KEY
ELEMENTS
	• **job title**: essentially used as a means of identification, but may carry implications for personnel matters and trade union membership
	• **duties and responsibilities**: these can be described in greater or lesser detail but provide, in even their most abbreviated form, a useful checklist when appointing a new supervisor or appraising the performance of an experienced supervisor. Such a checklist should provide some breakdown of the craft supervisory duties and responsibilities into:
	  – the amount and range of manual work expected
	  – the technical tasks required
	  – the essential administrative tasks
	  – the likely size and composition of the team for which the craft supervisor is responsible
	  – the level of management within an organization to which craft supervisors would be responsible
	• **skills and knowledge required**: these may include:
	  – essential qualifications
	  – previous participation in preferred training programmes such as a completed apprenticeship
	  – craft experience of specific types of work
	  – a clean driving licence
	  – attendance at recognized safety and first aid courses

- **working conditions**: may state:
  - where the job is located
  - whether it is site, workshop or office based
  - whether it involves considerable travelling
  - whether there are special working conditions which are different from other occupations within the organization
- the main **terms and conditions of employment** that relate specifically to the position of craft supervisor.

It is here necessary to draw a distinction between job descriptions and job guides which relate to the specific operational posts or positions within an organization, and the statements specifying the main terms and conditions of employment which the law requires to be given to every employee within 13 weeks of engagement.

The former relate to the structure and characteristics of the organization, the latter to the employment contracts of specific individuals within an organization.

THE NEED FOR ESTABLISHED OPERATING PROCEDURES

In a small organization each employee may have a certain amount of freedom in which to personalize the job. In larger organizations, where craft supervisors may be transferred from one project to another and therefore transfer their responsibilities from one part of the organization to another, there is considerable benefit in having reasonably standard operating procedures.

Difficulties can soon arise if there are no standard hours of work, and if only some supervisors report to a particular office or depot at regular times. Within construction there are a number of factors which make standardized operating procedures for all craft supervisors difficult to establish. It is therefore normal to consider standardizing procedures on only the larger projects in which several craft supervisors are simultaneously engaged with similarly sized teams on broadly identical work packages.

Mostly, the broad operating procedures adopted by each craft supervisor are negotiated between the individual supervisor, the work team and the manager to whom the supervisor is responsible.

RECORD SYSTEMS

Most supervisors will be expected to participate in establishing and maintaining some of the basic administrative and clerical records required in an efficient business organization. Only rarely will a craft supervisor have any clerical assistance, and many newly appointed supervisors find themselves unprepared for the amount of administrative work required of them.

The following is a list of some of the more common administrative processes which will require the attention of a craft supervisor at some time or other:

ADMINISTRA- TIVE PROCESSES	• checking or completing operatives' timesheets • preparing cutting lists or schedules of materials • preparing or checking materials requisitions • checking materials delivery notes at the time of delivery • checking invoices before payment is approved • preparing or checking plant and equipment requisitions • maintaining stockbooks • checking bonus sheets • checking entries in accident books • maintaining registers of appropriate inspections and tests • making daily or weekly reports on progress.

In many instances standard forms and procedures are available, such as time sheets, cutting lists, registers for inspections and daily report sheets, so the craft supervisor has some guidance on the kind of information that is required. Where the craft supervisor is required to provide specific information by agreed dates, on forms which provide guidance on the information needed, it is relatively easy to establish whether the task has been satisfactorily completed. Where the craft supervisor is required to check the accuracy of time sheets, invoices, bonus sheets and the entries in accident books, which have been made out by other people, it is less easy to establish how painstakingly the craft supervisor has completed the tasks.

THE NEED FOR REGULAR CHECKING OF PROCEDURES

All too often craft supervisors forget that they are part of a management chain which has a collective responsibility for the effectiveness of the organization. Most checking procedures are designed to identify and correct accidental errors and omissions. Occasionally a supervisor may discover that there have been apparently deliberate attempts to falsify records. Regular and diligent checking should identify such attempts before they have become major problem areas, allowing remedial action to be taken at an early stage.

Unfortunately many craft supervisors take the view that their job is only about the day-to-day supervision of the work of their team, and anything that gets in the way of this basic task is at best an inconvenience and at worst a major distraction. Many employers will, however, take the view that supervisors who continually operate outside the framework of their job guides, and who ignore the administrative requirements of their jobs, no matter how much attention they give to the supervision of the work or how skilled they are at their craft, are less than competent.

SUMMARY

First line supervisors seldom have opportunities to shape the organizational structure within which they work. However, they need to know something about the organizational culture and the policies which affect their work. Where there are job guides, clearly stated operating procedures and record systems it is easier for the newly appointed supervisor to become an effective part of the management team.

FURTHER STUDY OPPORTUNITIES

The following give a more detailed examination of the organizational framework within which first line supervisors operate:

HANDY, C. B., *Understanding organizations*, Penguin Books, 2nd edition 1981

KANAWATY, G., (ed) *Managing and Developing new forms of Work Organisation*, Management Development Series No 16 Geneva, Switzerland, ILO publications, 2nd revised edition 1989

MILLER, E. J., (ed) *Task and Organization*, John Wiley and Sons 1976

PUGH, D. S., (ed) *Organization Theory*, Penguin Books 1980

SALAMAN, G., and THOMPSON, K., *People and Organisations*, The Open University Press 1973

SILVERMAN, D., *The theory of Organisations*, Heinemann 1970

STEWART, P. H. and CANTOR, M. G., (eds) *Varieties of Work*, Sage Publications 1982

WILD, R., *Work Organization*, A study of manual work and mass production, John Wiley and Sons, 1975

CHAPTER THREE

THE CRAFT SUPERVISOR'S RESPONSIBILITIES IN OUTLINE

The first two chapters have introduced the industrial and organizational frameworks within which construction craft supervisors operate. This chapter outlines some of the supervisor's responsibilities that emerge as a consequence of operating within these frameworks. These responsibilities may be grouped, and linked with the supervision of the work, the team, and the workplace.

THE CONTEXT

Each supervisor has to shape broad, and often generally stated, responsibilities to meet the specific requirements of individual managers, projects, work teams and the individuals within those work teams, and the needs and potential hazards of each workplace. This is not an easy task, even when the supervisor is working within a relatively stable management and operational structure.

On some construction projects, the working environment, work teams and management structures can change significantly within the life of the project, thus making the supervisor's responsibilities more difficult to define with any clarity. Therefore one of the major challenges facing the craft supervisor is the need to maintain a clear picture of the responsibilities associated with the job against a background of changes in the nature of the workplace, work team, project and management structure.

THE CRAFT SUPERVISOR'S RESPONSIBILITIES FOR THE WORK

Construction work is project based and each project has its own unique characteristics. Sometimes these characteristics are striking and obvious and sometimes they are subtle and obscure. For instance, it may be obvious that the front entrance doors to a city centre bank require higher quality materials and workmanship than would be required for a farm outbuilding, but it may be less obvious that a client has very special requirements regarding the colour scheme in one room and no such special requirements about the remainder of the internal decorations.

ORDERS AND CONTRACTS

One of the main areas of craft supervisory responsibility is for that part of any project which provides work for the team. Almost without exception this work will be defined in an order or a contract. With larger projects these orders or contracts will be formalized by drawings, specifications or bills of quantities. With smaller projects there may be very few documents so that most of the work is agreed through discussion between the parties to the contract.

The law recognizes **oral** as well as **written** contracts, but it is much more difficult, some time after the event, to remember exactly what was agreed unless there is a written record. Therefore it is a well established principle always to have a written contract. Building contracts are complex. Almost any building law report highlights the complexity of the contractual issues. There are three crucial issues which need to be considered:

CRUCIAL CONTRACT- UAL ISSUES	• there are many different forms of contract for building work • the contract terms and conditions may be contained in many different documents • the contract documents may refer the parties to other documents which may not be readily available to the craft supervisor.

SELECTING THE FORM OF CONTRACT

A building contract is a legally binding agreement which is entered into between two parties; one of the parties being the client – usually called **the employer** – and the other party called **the contractor**. The employer may be the building owner, the main contractor or a sub-contractor. The contractor may be the main contractor, a sub-contractor or a supplier. Within this context, the craft supervisor is normally part of the contractor's organization.

The two parties to a building contract may sit down with a blank sheet of paper and write their own contract and this would be a perfectly legal thing to do. It might, however, present certain difficulties if the parties, at some later date, found themselves in dispute with each other, because the words which they used to describe their agreement may not have clear and unambiguous legal meaning.

For this reason there is a preference to use standard forms of building contracts. These are printed forms available within the industry which define the terms and conditions of the agreement which the parties have accepted as the basis of the contract. There are now many different standard forms of contract available, and most of them require the contract parties to choose between optional clauses and to make special entries regarding particular aspects of the agreement. This means that there can be very special contractual terms and conditions for projects which contain what appear to be similar types of work. It is therefore **dangerous** to assume that the contract terms on one project will be similar to the contract terms on any other project.

There are many instances where craft supervisors do not know which form of contract has been used for the project on which they are working. This means that on those projects craft supervisors may sometimes be working outside the terms of the contract, and thus place the contractor in breach of contract. For example, some standard forms of contract require the contractor to have a supervisor permanently on the site during the progress of the work so that the employer has a contractor's representative available at all reasonable times. Each craft supervisor should know when they are required to assume that particular contractual role, and if on any project they are not so required, then they should know what the formal route is for others to communicate with their organization regarding the contract works.

THE CONTRACT DOCUMENTS

The contractual requirements regarding a specific building project may be contained within many different documents. These may include:

POSSIBLE CONTRACT DOCUMENTS	
	• the written terms and conditions of the contract
	• drawings
	• specifications
	• bills of quantity
	• schedules
	• programmes of work
	• method statements
	• letters and written instructions.

Some of these documents may be contract documents and some may not. It is very important for the craft supervisor to know which are the contract documents.

The contract documents are those which both parties to the contract either incorporated within the contract at the start, or which the contract empowered them to issue during the progress of the works. This situation can best be illustrated by reference to drawings. Some of the drawings issued for a particular project will be **the contract drawings**, and these should be defined as such so that there is no doubt about the matter.

Other drawings may be issued during the progress of the works to **explain and amplify** the contract drawings, but these will not be contract drawings and they should not contain extra work, or omit or alter work which was part of the original contract. If any such drawing does show attempts to vary the terms of the original contract, then this should be queried before any action is taken.

Finally, drawings may be issued during the progress of the work which are intended to vary the terms and conditions of the original contract. They may omit, add to or vary any of the contract works and provide, in part, an instruction for the original contract to be varied. Therefore it is essential that a craft supervisor knows which drawings are:

DRAWINGS	• contract drawings • drawings which explain and amplify the contract drawings • drawings which constitute variations to the contract

because the craft supervisor's actions will be different in each case.

It is not an easy matter to keep track of contract documents, to identify which are contract documents and which are not, or to identify properly authorized variations to the contract, and in most cases the craft supervisor will require help from other members of the management team in this respect. The fundamental rule is for the craft supervisor to **look for discrepancies between documents** and, where these are found, to point them out, preferably in writing, and to ask for clarification. It is not correct to work from the latest information received, nor is it correct to assume that drawings take precedent over bills of quantity. Often the craft supervisor will find that only some of the contract documents have been made available because it may not be necessary for a craft supervisor to have a personal copy of every contract document.

However, the craft supervisor should know what documents are available and where they can be found if it is necessary to consult them during the progress of the work. On projects where there are many contract and supporting documents it is important for the craft supervisor to record exactly which documents have been received and when they were received.

REFERENCES TO OTHER DOCUMENTS

Finally, in this section, contract documents may make reference to other documents which are not readily available to the craft supervisor. The classic example is the reference within bills of quantity to British Standard Specifications and other documents. The following are illustrations taken from a bill of quantities:

REFERENCES TO BRITISH STANDARDS	• the sand for external renderings, internal cement plastering and internal lime undercoats shall comply with BS 1199, graded as Table 1

- particular care shall be taken before, during and after plastering in accordance with Clause 44 of BS 5492
- metal wall ties shall comply with BS 1243 and shall be of a type approved by the Engineer
- all materials shall be stored, measured, mixed and used in accordance with recognized good practice, as set out in BS 5492
- dividing strips between different floor finishes shall be of plastic of a colour to be approved by the architect
- the sealant shall be applied with a gun in accordance with the manufacturer's instructions
- the lime shall be hydrated lime obtained from an approved manufacturer and shall comply with BS 890
- bolts, screws, nuts and washers shall be of the type specified and shall be in accordance with the latest appropriate BS.

These referencess pose a number of different issues. The first, and most important issue, is whether the craft supervisor has ready access to current British Standard Specifications. Experience suggests that this is not the case. Secondly, it is reasonable to expect the Buying Department to ensure that materials are ordered to comply with British Standards, but it is not always clear how the craft supervisor is to ensure that the materials delivered to the site comply with those requirements. Thirdly, it is seldom the case that the manufacturer's instructions are obtained and passed to the first line supervisor early enough so that preparatory work meets the manufacturer's requirements.

WORKMANSHIP

The craft supervisor is in a very vulnerable position regarding workmanship issues, particularly those for which the contract documents make specific reference to British or other Standards or to manufacturers' recommendations. Where quality assurance is an issue, care should be taken to ensure that the craft supervisor is given all the appropriate information associated with the contract works. Traditionally this does not happen on most construction sites. It is usually only after a failure of some kind that British Standards and manufacturers' recommendations are obtained and compared with what was actually done.

THE CRAFT SUPERVISOR'S RESPONSIBILITIES FOR THE WORK TEAM

A craft supervisor's duties may include, among other things:

SOME SUPER-VISORY RESPONSI-BILITIES	• organizing the work team • allocating tasks to individual members of the team • allocating materials, plant and equipment • controlling production rates • controlling workmanship standards • controlling safety, health and welfare at the work place • keeping basic administrative records.

These responsibilities are principally matters associated with the effective allocation and control of resources. In principle this sounds straightforward, and many craft supervisors' job guides will state these basic responsibilities. There is no great difficulty in allocating equally interesting tasks to equally competent team members, in sharing appropriate resources fairly between individuals, or in recognizing obviously bad workmanship.

However, team members are not all equally competent, all tasks are not equally difficult or equally interesting, there may not be enough of the right resources to share between the members of the team as they would wish, and there might be very different views about what is an appropriate standard of workmanship to be expected from individuals with differing skills, knowledge and experience. Therefore the craft supervisor will most often have to think carefully before taking particular actions such as allocating work to specific individuals.

ALLOCATING TASKS TO TEAM MEMBERS

This seemingly simple process of allocating tasks to individual members of the team raises many issues for the first line supervisor. Answers to the following questions may help to make that process more effective:

MATTERS TO CONSIDER WHEN ALLOCATING TASKS	• does the supervisor understand the task which forms the basis of the instruction to the operative? • is the operative in a receptive frame of mind to receive the instruction? • can the instruction be given orally without risk of misinterpretation, or should it be reinforced with sketches or written information? • is the operative capable of carrying out the instruction with little risk of error? • is the work within the range of skill and ability of the operative?

- are there elements of the work which require special attention?
- are the necessary materials and equipment readily available to the operative?
- is there a preferred method of carrying out the work?
- will the job take a long time, in which case should the instructions be given in stages?
- are there special safety factors to be considered?
- how much supervision needs to be given whilst work is in progress?

In seeking to answer these, and similar questions, the craft supervisor will recognize what is involved in being located in that middle ground between management and operatives. Sometimes first line supervisors find themselves facing fundamental difficulties when attempting to make this link between management and operatives more effective. The difficulties which most frequently occur are when:

COMMON SUPERVISORY DIFFICULTIES

- managers do not keep the supervisor fully informed about all matters which concern either the members of the team or the individual supervisor
- managers expect the supervisor's full support for actions which they know are likely to be unpopular with members of the team
- the supervisor is persuaded by management to get team members to participate in unpopular activities
- the supervisor is unable to participate in activities which are exclusive to either managers or operatives
- individual team members do not inform the supervisor of all their work related activities
- members of the team expect the supervisor's support for activities they know are antagonistic to management.

EXPERIENCE OF TEAM WORKING

Thus the supervisor finds that what used to be simply called leadership is a complex combination of negotiating, broking, resource investigating and networking skills. These skills are usually learnt through experience of team working rather than through the accumulation of knowledge. Therefore carefully planned work experience is necessary for the development of effective skills in supervising work teams. During these periods of planned work experience, instances will arise when individual members of the team behave unpredictably.

COPING WITH UNPREDICTABLE BEHAVIOUR

Unpredictable behaviour by members of the work team presents the craft supervisor with a new set of challenges which may result in a need to reprimand a member of the team for an act of misconduct. There are detailed procedures associated with handling misconduct and these will be considered later. There is, however, a prior consideration for the craft supervisor. The following questions may need careful thought before the supervisor apportions blame:

THINK BEFORE APPOR- TIONING BLAME	<ul><li>did the operative understand the instruction or was there some misunderstanding about the action that was expected?</li><li>was the action required of the operative within that person's ability or was there a real risk of failure from the start through inexperience or lack of knowledge or skill?</li><li>was there firm evidence that the action, or lack of action, was linked with that individual member of the team?</li><li>was the individual known to be under any particular stress at the time?</li><li>was this an isolated instance, or had this happened before?</li><li>was the incident serious enough to fall within the category of acts for which employees have been notified in advance that dismissal would result?</li><li>was the individual provoked in any way?</li><li>were other members of the team involved?</li></ul>

Again these questions suggest that there might be a variety of reasons why individuals within a team do not always behave in predictable ways. It is important that the supervisor is able to distinguish between unpredictable actions by team members which were stimulated by misunderstanding, by ignorance, by stress, by provocation, by self interest or by team spirit. Thus the supervisor has to be sufficiently close to the action to see what is happening but also sufficiently detached that objective assessments can be made of the performance of individual members of the team and of the team as a whole.

THE CRAFT SUPERVISOR'S RESPONSIBILITIES FOR THE WORKPLACE

In the construction industry the workplace may be defined as: a workshop or factory, a construction site which is occupied solely by the main contractor and his sub-contractors, or an occupied building. There are significant differences associated with each of these settings which should be considered by craft supervisors.

THE WORKSHOP OR FACTORY

Where the workplace is a workshop or factory it can be assumed that this is controlled by the same organization as that which employs the craft supervisor and the work team. There is therefore no division of responsibility for the workplace. If the craft supervisor's job description states that the safety and security of the workshop is the responsibility of the craft supervisor then that is the sole responsibility of the craft supervisor. There may be specialized advice available but the responsibilities are clear and undivided.

THE CONSTRUCTION SITE

Where the workplace is a construction site then the craft supervisor may be in one of two possible positions; either directly employed as part of the main contractor's site management team, or working as the craft supervisor of a specialist team under a sub-contract arrangement with the main contractor. In the first case the craft supervisor is part of a management team covering the whole site; in the second case the craft supervisor has a responsibility only for those parts of the site allocated for the work of the sub-contractor.

In the second case it is essential that the craft supervisor and the work team know which areas of the site are available for either their sole use, or which are to be shared with other work teams. The craft supervisor will then have a responsibility to inform the main contractor of any hazards associated with their specialist work, which the main contractor should draw to the attention of other work teams using the same area of the site. In most cases sub-contractors are expected to share working places with other work teams and this can raise special problems regarding safety and security.

WORKING IN OCCUPIED PREMISES

Finally the craft supervisor and the work team may be required to work in occupied premises, that is to use work places which are not only shared by other construction workers but which are also in use by others as homes, offices, factories or places for public entertainment or rights of way during the progress of the work. Some construction teams, particularly those associated with mechanical and electrical services and with painting and decorating, have become particularly skilled in working in such places, but an increasing amount of construction work is taking place in occupied premises, introducing more and more construction workers and their supervisors to new working environments with additional hazards and security problems, not just for themselves but also for the occupants.

SUMMARY

Thus it can be seen that for each and every project it is necessary to consider the detailed craft supervisory responsibilities which arise jointly from the specific characteristics of the work team, the contract works and the workplace. Each project will present its own unique features which make the craft supervisor's job both immensely interesting and demanding.

FURTHER STUDY OPPORTUNITIES

BELBIN, R. MEREDITH, *Management teams* – why they succeed or fail, Heinemann Ltd 1981

BRITISH STANDARDS INSTITUTE, *Workmanship on building sites*, BS 8000 in 15 separate parts 1989 and 1990

DUNKERLEY, D., *The foreman*, Routledge and Kegan Paul 1975

FLEISHMAN, E. A., HARRIS, E. F., and BURTT, H. E., *Leadership and supervision in industry*, Columbus, Ohio State University 1955

I.L.O., *Modular programme for supervisory development*, 34 modules in a loose-leaf presentation arranged in 5 volumes – the volumes are **not** sold separately, International Labour Organization, 4th impression 1984

MANSON, K. and HARLOW, P, *Contracts and building law review*, Chartered Institute of Building 1986 with Supplements

MINISTRY OF LABOUR, *The training of supervisors*, A report of a report of a Committee of Inquiry, HMSO 1954

N.I.I.P., *The foreman*, A study of supervision in British Industry undertaken by the National Institute of Industrial Psychology, Staples Press 1951

N.I.I.P., *The place of the foreman in management*, Seven case studies undertaken by the National Institute of Industrial Psychology, Staples Press 1957

SEEL, C., *Contractual procedures for building students*, London, Holt, Rinehart and Winston 1984

THURLEY, K. E. and HAMBLIN, A. C., *The supervisor and his job*, HMSO 1958

THURLEY, K. and WIRDENIUS, H., *Approaches to supervisory development*, Institute of Personnel Management 1973

VAN DERSAL, W. R., *The Successful Supervisor*, Pitman 1970

WIRDENIUS, H. and LONNSJO, S., *Functions of supervisors in the building industry*, Stockholm, Sweden, The National Swedish Council for Building Research 1964

CHAPTER FOUR

COLLABORATION WITH OTHER WORK TEAMS

In this chapter consideration will be given to four main issues; the opportunities which are available for liaison with other supervisors, the considerations which arise when several work teams need to operate within a common working area, concern for the hazards associated with the work of each team and the use of method statements and programmes of work as a means of recording any agreements which have been reached.

TEAMWORK

Construction requires teamwork. Not just teamwork within one specific team, but collaboration with all those other teams sharing the same workplace or whose work or methods of working may, to some extent or other, affect the performance of a supervisor's team. Sometimes all these work teams may be part of the same organization, but normally some of them will belong to other organizations with which there may be no direct contractual relationships. Thus the outcome of any collaboration between supervisors, whether positive and beneficial or negative and restrictive, is likely to be a direct consequence of the personal negotiating skills of each.

THE OPPORTUNITIES FOR LIAISON WITH OTHER SUPERVISORS

These fall into two main groups; the relatively formal opportunities which are associated with contractual and project arrangements, and the informal opportunities which arise during the progress of the work.

FORMAL OPPORTUNITIES FOR LIAISON

Contractually, there are two main formal opportunities for collaboration:

OPPORTUN-ITIES FOR COLLABORA-TION	• when the supervisor's work team is part of a direct contractual arrangement with another organization • when the work teams meet regularly, at the request of the site or project management, to monitor

and evaluate progress and to prepare future short term programmes of work.

Where there are direct contractual relationships, it is usual for the nature and quantity of the work to be stated in some detail, together with proposed start and completion dates. Financial issues will also be stated including the contract sum and the arrangements for measuring work satisfactorily completed, for stage and final payments, for retention monies and for making good any defects which appear during the defects liability period. There are, however, other issues which, if considered and agreed at the pre-contract stage, make the collaboration with other work teams easier for the individual supervisor once work has started. These issues include the following:

ISSUES TO DISCUSS WITH OTHER SUPERVISORS	• the sequence in which the work will be carried out • whether the work will be carried out as one continuous programme or whether there will be periods when there will be no work in progress. • whether one supervisor will be responsible for the whole project, or whether there will be different work teams, and therefore different supervisors, working on particular stages of the work • the arrangements to be made for the unloading, site storage and handling of materials • the arrangements to be made for sharing plant and site services, and the extent to which other work teams will be bringing their own plant, equipment and temporary buildings • the extent to which the work of other teams must be completed before the work in question can start • crucial dates by which sections or stages of the work must be completed to allow access for following work teams • responsibilities for removing rubbish and surplus materials and plant from the work areas • responsibilities for protecting completed work from damage.

There are many instances where most of these issues have been agreed at the **pre-contract stage** and have been incorporated into the contract documents. But sometimes craft supervisors will not have been informed of the precise contract details, and as a consequence many carefully agreed and sensible arrangements will have been ignored during the progress of the work. There are also many instances where such matters have not been given adequate consideration at the pre-contract stage, and craft supervisors are left to make all the necessary arrangements for themselves during the progress of the work.

Many of the items in the above list may have **cost implications**, and craft supervisors must always be alert to the possibility that their negotiations may result in higher costs for their employer. So it is vital that craft supervisors are informed of the terms and conditions of the contracts which are their responsibility, and of the areas where they are expected to make their own site arrangements through liaison with other supervisors.

SITE MEETINGS

On many larger construction projects there will be regular site or project meetings to which representatives of all the principal participating organizations are invited and expected to attend. It is usual for all the work teams whose work is about to start to be invited as well as those currently working on the project. It is good practice, but regretfully this is not always followed, for the craft supervisor of each work team to be present in addition to any more senior management representatives. The objectives of such meetings include:

OBJECTIVES OF SITE MEETINGS	• reviewing the progress achieved to date in each specified area of work • identifying problem areas, unforeseen difficulties or other matters affecting the progress or quality of the work • programming the work for the next stage or work period.

With the more efficient project or site management teams the objectives of these meetings will be agreed in advance, agendas will be prepared and specific individuals will be invited to attend. Where this is the case the individual craft supervisor, if invited, has time to prepare documentation on progress and any problems which currently exist and strategies for the future. In such preparations the craft supervisor may need to consider the following:

SITE MEET-INGS – PRIOR CONSIDERA-TIONS	• the requirements of the contract or order • the original programme of work • the resources considered necessary to meet the original programme • any changes that have had to be made in the work • the extent to which these changes have been properly authorized • whether extensions of time or increases in cost have been awarded or are appropriate

- a summary of the resources which are or have been used, including:
  - manpower
  - materials
  - plant and equipment
- identify any shortages of:
  - manpower
  - materials
  - plant and equipment
  - information
  - sub-contractors
- whether there have been any delays in progress and if so what the reasons were for these delays
- identify opportunities to improve progress through:
  - working overtime
  - additional manpower
  - additional materials
  - additional plant and equipment
  - provision of outstanding information
  - proposals for revisions to working methods
- the preparation of realistic targets for those aspects of the work which are to feature in the next programming period.

One of the main difficulties which arise during these meetings is the tendency for the representatives of some participating teams to blame others for any delays in, or problems with, the work. Where a craft supervisor is of the opinion that the progress or quality of the work has been adversely affected by the actions or lack of action of other participants, then the issues should be talked through beforehand with those concerned. If this is done, then none of the participants directly associated with the issues need be surprised by statements made at formal meetings when minutes will be taken and remedial actions suggested. Therefore it is important to recognize that liaison with other supervisors is easier when formal meetings are preceded by informal discussions aimed at establishing the facts and the needs and interests of each work team.

INFORMAL OPPORTUNITIES FOR LIAISON

Informal meetings should be seen as an essential element in the process of liaison with other supervisors. Broadly there are two strategies which can be used; establishing a regular pattern of informal meetings at the beginning of each working day or week, or arranging meetings only when they are considered necessary. Both strategies need to be thought through carefully. Regular meetings with no particular purpose can be time wasting, and meetings which are called only when necessary can lead to the view that, 'He only comes to see me when he wants something'. Therefore informal meetings between supervisors should be used as a means of sharing information through genuine two-way communications rather than as an opportunity for presenting a list of demands. Some of the issues which might be considered during such meetings include:

SOME ISSUES FOR INFORMAL MEETINGS	• talking through the preferred sequences of working • factors influencing continuity of work • arrangements for the use of shared plant, equipment and welfare accommodation • anticipated completion dates for specific stages of the work • protective measures that might concern other work teams • instances where attention might need to be directed to particular issues, such as dimensional tolerance problems, difficulties regarding access to the workplace.

In order to keep these meetings informal it is wise to avoid approaching other supervisors with a written list of issues to discuss and resolve. It will be necessary to plan out in advance what needs to be said, and some preparatory investigation might be necessary, and afterwards some record of what was discussed and agreed might be made in the site diary, but the meetings themselves should enable the issues to be explored freely by all participants without the constraints of an agenda and minutes.

There are two particular sets of issues where informal liaison between craft supervisors may be of considerable benefit; these are where two or more teams are required to share the same working area, and where there are particular hazards associated with the work of one or more teams.

SHARING COMMON WORKING AREAS

Ideally most supervisors would welcome a situation in which they did not have to share any working area with another work team. Usually it is possible to prevent access to workplaces by others only when the hazards associated with the work in progress are so great that personal injury is a real risk. Demolition is a classic example of an operation where other work teams should be kept well away from the area where the work is taking place. In most other situations it is usual for different work groups to share workplaces. There are a number of reasons why shared workplaces might be preferred:

REASONS FOR SHARING WORKPLACES	• the work teams are kept together and do not get spread out over the whole site or building • the work is easier to supervise by the main contractor or project manager • nuisance to others can be restricted • a smaller area of the site has to be serviced with temporary power, lighting, materials and stores, scaffolding and other access equipment and mechanical plant • less clearing-up and security checks are required at the end of each work period.

Where the working area is small and congested, where the building is occupied or open to the public, where the work teams are large, and the nature of the work is changing rapidly, then collaboration with other work teams will be essential. There are a number of special issues which should be considered in addition to those already raised. These include:

ISSUES TO CONSIDER WHEN SHARING WORKPLACES	• the location of storage areas for each work group • the maximum amounts of materials that may be brought into the workplace at any one time • the maximum and minimum team sizes that can be accommodated without particular inconvenience to others • anticipated progress of work and any attendance required by other teams • the particular sequence in which each team will work in order to maximize their own performance and to minimize problems for others • the identification of areas in which special hazards exist • the precautions which should be taken to minimize risk and inconvenience to others • areas where preparatory work, such as setting out, has to be agreed with several supervisors before work can start.

HAZARDS ASSOCIATED WITH THE WORK

The principal reason for not encouraging shared working areas is concerned with the **special hazards** that might be associated with the work of any team. Attention will be paid to safety issues later, but here it is necessary to emphasize that craft supervisors must not only be concerned with the safety of their own team members but also with others who share the working area, who might be members of the public, occupants of the building or the direct responsibility of other craft supervisors. It is this last group that provides a major need as well as an opportunity for collaboration with the supervisors of other work teams.

It is obvious that the members of a particular work team, especially the supervisor of that team, appreciate better than anyone else the hazards that are associated with their work and the precautions that need to be taken to minimize the risk of accidents. It is, however, not always appreciated that others who share the same workplace may not have the same understanding of either the hazards or the precautions to be taken. This means that before work starts, and especially before the start of any particularly hazardous task, it is important that the appropriate first line supervisor alerts all others with supervisory responsibilities in the area of the nature of the hazards and the precautions to be taken.

Where the hazards are obvious and the risk of serious injury high, as for example where one team requires the guards to be removed from machinery so that they can carry out essential repair work, other work teams should be excluded from the area of high risk. Where this is not possible, because of the nature of the work involved, then the appropriate supervisors must collaborate to such an extent that there is agreement regarding the:

ISSUES TO BE AGREED WHEN SHARING WORKPLACES	• exact nature of the work involved and the appropriate method of working • skills and experience appropriate for those working in the area on the particular task • hazards associated with the work • precautions that must be taken to minimize the risk of accidents • which supervisor has overall responsibility for co-ordinating the work.

Where particularly hazardous work has to be undertaken in areas accessible to the public or in occupied buildings, then the craft supervisor must ensure that adequate protection is provided, and the simplest way of doing this may be to keep members of the public, occupants or visitors away from the immediate area of the work.

METHOD STATEMENTS AND PROGRAMMES OF WORK

The most likely outcome of collaboration with supervisors of other work teams will mean small, but highly significant, changes in the agreements regarding the method of work, the layout of the workplace and the shared use of scaffolding, plant and other project facilities. It is insufficient for these agreements to be made between supervisors; the members of each work team will also have to modify their preferred methods of working to accommodate the terms of these agreements. Therefore it is important that each supervisor communicates effectively with the individual members of the team so that the appropriate actions are taken at the agreed times and in the agreed sequence.

The subject of supervisory communication skills will be considered in more detail in the next chapter, but here it is necessary to emphasize that the outcome of meetings with other supervisors regarding shared working areas, and the precautions to be taken against any special hazards associated with the work, should best be incorporated within:

- **simple written method statements**, such as a list of the tasks to be undertaken in the agreed sequence, with notes on the method of working, on the equipment required and on the time each phase of the work is expected to take
- **detailed programmes of work**, which might take the form of a bar chart or a flow diagram for the team with any special features of the work described in more detail.

All the benefits of collaboration with other work teams and liaison with other supervisors may be wasted unless the outcomes are effectively applied by the members of each team. Effective communication skills are therefore essential, together with the recognition that it may be necessary for the whole team or some members of the team to work in a different sequence from their normal pattern of working, and such changes need careful explanation and recognition by the team when there are valid reasons why such changes are necessary.

SUMMARY

Construction work is most effective when based on teamwork. Teamwork involves collaboration within and between teams. Craft supervisors have opportunities for collaborating with other work teams through formal site or project meetings and through informal meetings with other supervisors.

Liaison with other work teams is of particular importance when two or more teams are expected to share the same working area and where there are particular hazards associated with the work of one or more teams.

Method statements and work programmes are the most obvious forms in which the outcome of collaboration can be summarized and presented.

FURTHER STUDY OPPORTUNITIES

The following give a more detailed examination of the issues associated with team work:

ARGYLE, M., *The Social Psychology of Work*, Penguin Books 1972

BELBIN, R. MEREDITH, *Management Teams* – why they succeed or fail, William Heinemann 1981

JANIS, I. L., *Victims of Group Think*, Boston, Mass, Houghton Mifflin 1972

JAY, A., *Management and Machiavelli*, Penguin Books 1967

RACKHAM, N., HONEY, P. and COLBERT, M. J., *Developing Interactive Skills*, Wellens Publishing 1971

CHAPTER FIVE

RECORDS AND COMMUNICATIONS

This chapter will concentrate on the records associated with the progress of work, with contractual matters and with statutory requirements; on written and oral communications, and on formal and informal meetings.

Many newly appointed construction craft supervisors are surprised by the amount of paperwork associated with their job. It is necessary to remember therefore that the craft supervisor is not only concerned with the day to day supervision of the work but is an essential link in the management structure of the organization in which the team and the supervisor are both employed. Therefore lack of proper attention to paperwork and communications by the craft supervisor means that there is an inadequate picture of matters which are of concern to the team and others in the organization. The craft supervisor has to develop skills in three broad areas: record keeping, communications with individuals, and in group meetings.

PROGRESS RECORDS
Most organizations require their site based first line supervisors to maintain regularly and hand in some formal records of progress. These records may take one of three main forms:

THE CRUCIAL PROGRESS RECORDS	• job tickets • daily or weekly report sheets • diaries.

JOB TICKETS
Where the work involves many small jobs at different locations, such as maintenance or repair work, it is usually easier to use a record system which is job based. Therefore a supervisor will often be required to complete a job ticket for each separate task showing:

JOB TICKETS SHOULD SHOW . . .	• when the work was completed • which team members worked on the job • how much time each person spent on the job

- what materials were used
- what plant was used.

With maintenance and repair work a supervisor may be required to complete many such job tickets in the course of a working week. Most tasks will present few problems. However, some will require special attention, particularly in those instances where extra work or materials have to be used to finish the job in addition to those stated on the job ticket, where the ticket provides an inaccurate or incomplete description of the work which has to be done, or where the job requires the attention of other work teams before it can be completed.

With job ticket work, it is essential that the supervisor pays particular attention to these 'specials', which normally only form a small percentage of the work completed in any one week, but which may take considerable supervisory effort to process. There are two areas which have traditionally presented organizations with problems. First, in many instances completed job tickets do not show all the materials used and do not describe all the work done, particularly where the original description is inadequate. Secondly, the job tickets for those jobs which cannot be completed by one team are often not passed on speedily to the following teams, causing unnecessary delay in the completion of the work.

DAILY OR WEEKLY REPORT SHEETS

With larger building projects, where the work team will be site based for some time, it is usual for the craft supervisor to complete regularly and submit standard daily or weekly report sheets. These records are designed so that each supervisor is required to provide, at regular intervals, specific information about the progress of the work. A standard report form might require the supervisor to include the following information:

REPORT
SHEETS
SHOULD
SHOW . . .

- the name of the project or site address
- the period (day or week) covered by the report
- the names of, and hours worked by, each team member on the project
- materials or equipment delivered to the site during the period
- a description of the work completed during the period
- delays and the reasons for each delay
- a description of any problems encountered during the period
- lists of materials, plant or instructions required.

The last four items on this list cause most problems, principally because they require thought and careful wording. Progress records should not be seen as something to be done in an odd moment, they should form part of the normal day's work of each supervisor, and progress records must be given appropriate time and attention.

DIARIES

With the smaller or less structured organization there may be no preferred report forms. In which case each craft supervisor should keep a personal record of progress. Personal records have both advantages and disadvantages. A personal record can be written in a less formal style and can include confidential comments and observations because it will not be seen by others. The disadvantages are that being a personal and confidential diary it should not be left lying about for anyone else to read. Also a personal record requires personal discipline, it is all too easy to discontinue entries when life is hectic or when the issues are complex and require careful thought. The discipline associated with the use of a standard report form, and the need to send a copy to head office at the end of each week, provides an organizational structure within which each supervisor is required to work.

CONTRACTUAL RECORDS

There are contractual records which many first line supervisors will need to keep, or to consider keeping, at some time in their career, these include:
- drawing registers
- oral and written instructions
- confirmation of oral instructions

DRAWING REGISTERS

The larger construction projects generate many drawings and these must be managed effectively by the craft supervisors involved. There are four principal issues to consider:

ISSUES TO CONSIDER WHEN RECORDING DRAWINGS	• drawings may come from several sources • they may supersede drawings which are already in use • they may provide information which conflicts with information previously received • some of the information on some drawings may need to be communicated to other people.

The craft supervisor should keep accurate records which show:

DRAWING REGISTERS SHOULD SHOW . . .	• when information, such as drawings and written site instructions, was received • who provided that information • a brief description of the information provided

- the number of copies of each drawing or written instruction received
- whether the drawing or written instruction supersedes any previous drawing or instruction
- whether any information contained on the drawing or in the written instruction conflicts with other contractual documents
- whether work already completed has been rendered obsolete by new instructions
- whether copies of the drawings or written instructions have to be sent to other people or organizations.

This whole area of contractual records is complex and does not receive sufficient attention generally within the industry. The craft supervisor must keep sufficient records to control the use of drawings, and in order to do so will need to check each drawing and instruction immediately upon receipt, to ensure that there are no major discrepancies between new instructions and work in progress.

Many organizations provide drawing registers so that basic data is easily recorded, but the first line supervisor will always have to check the contents of drawings and instruction to ensure that any superseded drawings are withdrawn from circulation, and that discrepancies and inconsistencies are identified and drawn to the attention of the appropriate person at the earliest moment. Oral instructions, however, provide the greatest problem area.

ORAL AND WRITTEN INSTRUCTIONS

The craft supervisor will need to know which persons have the power to issue instructions that can influence the terms and conditions of the contract, because those persons may occasionally decide to change the contract terms by issuing oral instructions.

Oral instructions are open to misinterpretation. To avoid this it is common practice, if at all possible, to ensure that they are confirmed in writing before any action is taken. It is preferable if the person issuing the oral instruction is also the person who confirms the instruction in writing because this simplifies the process. Where this cannot be arranged and the oral instruction has to be confirmed by the receiver – which may be the craft supervisor – this must be done speedily and action on the instruction delayed until the person giving the oral instruction has had a reasonable chance to check the accuracy of the written confirmation. Of course, in an emergency it would not be reasonable to wait until receiving confirmation of an oral instruction before taking appropriate action.

It is often difficult for the craft supervisor to know when to act immediately on an oral instruction, when to question the validity of a written instruction or when to raise a discrepancy between different instructions. This is an area in which it is very easy to be wise after the event. If there is any doubt about whether any special action is required then the craft supervisors should get specialist advice from their safety officer or senior manager.

STATUTORY RECORDS

Craft supervisors may have a responsibility to keep relevant statutory safety registers, or to see that such records are properly kept by others. This is particularly important for matters which may have a bearing upon the health or safety of members of the work team. The most common statutory registers with which craft supervisors might become involved are:

STATUTORY REGISTERS	• F 36 General Register for Building Operations and Works of Engineering Construction
	• BI 510A Accident book
	• F 91 (Part I) Records of Weekly Inspections, Examinations and Special Tests of:
	  – scaffolding
	  – excavations
	  – lifting appliances
	• F 91 (Part II) Record of Reports
	• F 2202 Register and Certificates of Shared Welfare Arrangements
	• F 2346 Register for the purposes of the Abrasive Wheels Regulations 1970.

It is essential that each craft supervisor establishes beyond reasonable doubt that all appropriate statutory records have been properly maintained. Where there is doubt then first line supervisors should confer with their safety officers or senior managers.

WRITTEN AND ORAL COMMUNICATIONS

From time to time craft supervisors will have to write letters and hold personal discussions with individuals which deal with important and perhaps confidential matters and usually there will be no secretary to help! With written communications there are a number of basic rules:

WRITTEN COMMUNICA-TIONS – THE RULES	• where a permanent record of the message is required the communication should be written rather than spoken • the words used should be understandable to the reader • important letters and reports normally require careful preparation, editing and revision before the meaning is really clear

> • if the communication might impose financial or legal commitments, then clearance should be obtained from senior management before the letter or report is sent.

Many organizations use standard letters for commonly occurring instances where the wording is important, and care is often taken to ensure that contractually significant letters are seen by the heads of the relevant departments before they are sent.

The craft supervisor is, however, not only concerned with writing letters and reports for others but also has to read and regularly refer to letters and reports prepared by others in order to keep fully informed. Thus reading and filing take up an appreciable amount of a craft supervisor's week.

By far the most common form of communication for craft supervisors is **oral communication**. This does not mean that it is less important or that it requires less thought than written communication. However, it probably does mean that there is more chance of misunderstanding because of the lack of a permanent record. Therefore the supervisor needs to consider several factors before speaking to someone else about important issues:

ORAL COMMUNICATIONS: SOME PRIOR CONSIDERATIONS	• whether the person being spoken to is in the right frame of mind to receive the message
	• when is the most appropriate time to give the message to obtain the maximum impact
	• whether the message is clearly and simply structured so that it is easy to understand
	• whether important elements within the message should be reinforced with diagrams or demonstrations
	• whether the message should be broken down into smaller elements, with each element given separately, so that there is less to remember
	• how to get the recipient of the message to repeat the salient elements so that errors or omissions can be identified and corrected
	• whether the message should be repeated on a later occasion
	• when is the most appropriate time to check whether the message has been translated into appropriate action.

There are often occasions when it is sensible to keep a record of when important oral messages were given and to whom they were given. The most obvious examples are:

ORAL COM- MUNICATIONS – WHEN RECORDS ARE NEEDED	• the verbal warnings given to individual members of the team about matters of workmanship and conduct • requests made to other supervisors for information or actions such as clearing an area so that your team can start work • telephone requests to staff at head office to chase the delivery of plant or materials, or the supply of additional information or resources.

It is recommended that important oral messages, those received and given, should be recorded in a personal job diary. It is often difficult to judge at the time whether a message is sufficiently important to be recorded in this way, and sometimes the real significance of a message only becomes apparent a long time after it was received. However, the discipline of spending just a few moments each day reflecting on the events of the previous day, before making a simple record of what are judged to be the most significant matters, is often well rewarded in the future. The records can be simple, such as:

Thursday 18 May
- 'spoke to X about timekeeping'
- 'spoke to the plasterer foreman about clearing his rubbish from room 123'
- 'phoned buying department about the non delivery of timber promised for today'
- 'reminded the general foreman that we will need access to the third floor on Monday'
- 'contracts manager told me that we were likely to be moved from this site in a week or two, seemed to think we knew this – first I've heard of it.'

MEETINGS

It is very easy to spend too much time in meetings which are either completely unnecessary or which take far longer than they need. Meetings involve bringing a group of people together so that views about a subject can be discussed and modified, so that a plan of action can be prepared and agreed following the collection of information and opinions from several people, or so that a prepared statement can be presented simultaneously to a group of people. Meetings should therefore have clear aims, such as:

MEETINGS – THEIR AIMS	• the sharing of information followed by the collective agreement and acceptance of a preferred course of action • the communication of vital and urgent information which may need supplementary explanation.

There are **formal** and there are **informal** meetings.

Formal meetings

Formal meetings tend to have rules, regarding such matters as:

RULES FOR MEETINGS SHOULD COVER . . .	• the agenda, distributed in advance, of the items of business to be dealt with during the meeting • those invited or required to attend, or to receive reports following, the meeting • the presentation of reports or written documents for consideration at the meeting • the conduct of business during the meeting • the distribution of minutes following the meeting.

Formal meetings require considerable preparation by those with responsibilities for **organizing** them, those required to **prepare reports** or written documents for them, and those required to attend them. Craft supervisors usually find themselves in the last of these three groups, that is they are sometimes required to **attend** formal meetings, and this means reading the documents sent out in advance and preparing for any discussions which might take place around any of the items on the agenda.

Consider the following agenda item:

To identify the reasons for the delay to the services on the third floor of the North Block and to agree a revised programme necessary to bring this work back onto programme during the next four weeks.

A craft supervisor with one of the sub-contractors responsible for the installation of the services on this site might consider the following actions as preparation for the meeting:

PREPARATION FOR SITE MEETINGS	• obtain and study a copy of the original contract or order for the work to the North Block
	• obtain and study a copy of the original programme of work for the installation of services in this block
	• obtain details of the resources originally considered necessary to meet the original programme of work
	• identify any changes that have had to be made in the work
	• establish the extent to which these changes have been properly authorized
	• establish whether extensions of time or increases in cost have already been awarded or are appropriate
	• establish the reasons for the delays
	• be prepared to summarize the resources already used under convenient headings such as:
	  – labour
	  – materials
	  – plant and equipment

- identify any current shortages in:
  - labour strength
  - materials
  - plant and equipment
  - information
  - the output of own sub-contractors
- check the accuracy of the above with senior managers and specialists within the company
- find out who else will be attending the meeting from your company and check the facts with them
- identify opportunities which might exist or the actions which will be required to bring the work back onto programme:
  - proposed revisions to working methods or sequence of working
  - additional information required
  - work necessary to be completed by others before further installation work can be done
  - additional plant and equipment required to speed up progress
  - additional materials required or the re-scheduling of deliveries required
  - additional labour required or overtime necessary and the implications arising from this.

This list shows that to be properly prepared for just one item on the agenda can take many hours and involve much collaboration with others. The consequences, however, of attending a meeting without being properly prepared are that assumptions may be made and promises given which cannot then be honoured. Care must always be taken to ensure that commitments are not made at meetings which involve company policy and which have not been checked out and agreed before the meeting starts. The most common mistakes in this respect are:

MEETINGS – SOME COMMON MISTAKES	<ul><li>promising additional labour, plant or equipment which is not forthcoming</li><li>agreeing delivery or partial completion dates which cannot be met</li><li>agreeing to work overtime without first clearing this with the team and with the firm.</li></ul>

Many formal site meetings do not provide for the attendance and participation of first line supervisors, and this raises the possibility that those who do attend will, through ignorance of the day-to-day project details, commit the craft supervisor and the team to a work programme which just cannot be met. It is therefore essential that before the meeting starts, the supervisor, with special responsibility for the craft or work 'parcel', briefs those attending so that they are properly prepared. All too often this is not done, with serious consequences.

Informal meetings

There are also many instances where informal meetings take place. These can have several potential disadvantages:

INFORMAL MEETINGS – DISADVAN-TAGES	• those who should attend are just not available • issues are not given proper consideration through lack of preparation and available information • there is no record of what was agreed, and those attending may take away different perceptions of what was agreed, or what action was to be taken.

However, informal meetings are useful, especially for:

INFORMAL MEETINGS – ADVANTAGES	• identifying potential or actual problem areas • exploring possible remedies • identifying preferred solutions to particular problems • establishing areas of concern • reviewing progress informally • evaluating performance • giving recognition for a task well done.

There are a few basic rules, even about informal meetings, which are worth considering:

INFORMAL MEETINGS – BASIC RULES	• keep them short but at the same time allow everyone enough time to make a thoughtful contribution • choose convenient times, not everyone supports meetings at lunch time or after work or at 7.30 in the morning, and whilst they may attend they may also not be in an appropriate frame of mind • don't use meetings to pick on individual members of the team • think carefully about how the views of each person present can be sought without embarrassment • keep the range of issues short and the presentation simple • if an issue is 'not negotiable' then say so as soon as possible, otherwise time can be wasted and frustration grow because the suggestions made cannot be implemented

> - consider who should be attending, but isn't, so that they can be seen separately afterwards
> - consider the need for a note which summarizes the main points to be distributed following the meeting
> - make it clear at the outset whether the issues being discussed are confidential or not.

Remember that all meetings cost money. It is worth just occasionally calculating the cost of all the time spent by those attending and then asking the question, 'Was it really worth while?'

SUMMARY

Craft supervisors will generally be required to complete job tickets, daily or weekly reports or job diaries as their part in recording the progress of the work. Craft supervisors may also need to keep drawing registers, records of written instructions received and confirmations of oral instructions as their contribution to contract administration. In addition craft supervisors need to maintain, or to see that others maintain on their behalf, statutory records of inspections, tests and examinations. All craft supervisors will have some involvement in written and oral communications such as letter and report writing, filing, records of verbal instructions received and given and involvement in formal and informal meetings. For some first line supervisors these administrative activities form a major part of the job.

FURTHER STUDY OPPORTUNITIES

The following give further opportunities to consider communication issues:

AUSTEN, A. D. and NEALE, R. H., *Managing Construction Projects*, A guide to processes and procedures, Geneva, Switzerland, International Labour Office 1984

BUTLER, J. T., *Elements of Administration for Building Students*, Hutchinson, 3rd edition 1982

DARBYSHIRE, A. E., *Report Writing*, The form and style of efficient communication, Edward Arnold 1970

HIGGIN, G. and JESSOP, N., *Communications in the Building Industry*, Tavistock Publications, 1965

PATERSON, J., *Information Methods for Design and Construction*, John Wiley and Sons, 1977

WILLIAMS, R., *Communications*, Penguin Books, 3rd edition 1976

CHAPTER SIX

THE EFFECTIVE USE OF HUMAN RESOURCES

This chapter is concerned with the role of the first line supervisor in developing the effective use of human resources within the work team. The issues that influence the performance of individual members of the team and of the team as a whole, and which are of particular concern to craft supervisors, include: recruitment and selection, the induction of new team members, motivation, career development, the constructive use of trade union representatives, and the ways in which first line supervisors address matters such as grievances, disputes and indiscipline.

Normally, a newly appointed supervisor takes over an existing team which has been developed by someone else. It is unusual for a supervisor to have the opportunity and freedom to construct a completely new work team. Therefore in most cases the existing members of the team will have already established their own attitudes and preferred ways of working before the new supervisor arrives, and these must be taken into account when seeking to improve performance and change patterns of behaviour. As a consequence there is no obvious starting point for making a more effective use of the human resources available to the supervisor. Each of the following issues provides the supervisor with an opportunity for improving performance. Handled badly, with inadequate preparation and thought and without sufficient attention to established attitudes, the consequences can so easily be a marked deterioration in performance and goodwill. Therefore, as each of the following issues arises the first line supervisor will need to consider how best to use that opportunity to make a positive contribution to the performance of the team and its members.

THE RECRUITMENT AND SELECTION OF NEW TEAM MEMBERS

From time to time opportunities will arise to bring new members into the team. These new team members may be apprentices, young craftsmen and women, experienced operatives, labourers or semi-skilled workers. Usually new team members are required either because someone is leaving the team, or because the work load has increased and a larger team is needed to cope with the extra work. In either case the supervisor will need to consider how the opportunity to introduce a new team member can be used to make the most beneficial effect upon the performance of the whole team. It may be possible to involve the team in discussions regarding the type of employee preferred, for example apprentice, labourer, or experienced craftsman. However, there may be organizational policies regarding new appointments and the employment of apprentices and trainees, which limit the opportunities for work team discussions.

It is therefore important for the supervisor to establish where opportunities exist for team discussions and where organizational policy restricts local decision making. For instance, if the organization has decided to reduce the overall size of its work force, the only opportunity to replace a team member who is leaving may be by internal transfer. The organization may have established central policies regarding the recruitment of trainees which do not provide opportunities for local initiatives. In such cases the supervisor has to be careful not to raise the expectations of the team in ways that are contrary to organizational policy.

METHODS OF RECRUITMENT

Once a decision has been made to recruit a new team member, attention should be directed to the appropriate method of recruitment. There are many approaches to recruitment including personal contacts, local advertisements, local recruitment campaigns and national recruitment programmes. The team members can play an important part in local recruitment campaigns through personal contacts. In such instances it is important that some guidance is given regarding job descriptions, and the ways in which interested persons should make their applications known to the organization. In the larger organizations these issues are usually the subject of established procedures, and difficulties arise where the procedures are not properly followed. With smaller organizations, where recruitment is much more likely to be through personal contact, it may be appropriate to consider the incentives which might influence someone's decision to seek, or to respond to an offer of, employment. These incentives include the obvious issues of pay and working conditions but they may also include opportunities for developing new skills, for career advancement or for participating in particularly high quality or otherwise interesting work. Therefore where the team members might be involved in recruitment matters, there are issues to be talked through and procedures to be established so that potential recruits are not frustrated by delays and uncertainties regarding their application for a job.

METHODS OF SELECTION

It is also important to recognize that there are several different methods of selection which might be used once applications are received for specific vacancies. These include interviews, skill and aptitude tests, and references from previous employers and from schools and colleges. Usually, there is a need to provide a range of personal details on an application form. These forms are carefully designed to establish:

PERSONAL DETAILS	• age • personal details • health, including sickness and disability records • appropriate qualifications • appropriate previous work experience • personal interests and career intentions.

Formal and detailed application forms are often seen as more appropriate for:

APPLICATION FORMS ARE MORE SUITABLE FOR . . .	• the selection of young people • those occupations for which specific training is considered necessary • where particular disabilities might be problematic • where new employees might be required to work in sensitive areas such as occupied buildings.

The submission of formal applications is then typically followed by one or more interviews or test sessions to which the first line supervisor may or may not be invited.

However, for many manual occupations in the construction industry selection methods have been rudimentary. This is because the industry has historically used 'casual' employment policies for hourly paid employees. Thus, rather than spend time and resources on interviews, selection tests and seeking references from previous employers, the preferred approach has been to employ the first likely applicants and to use the first few hours or days of employment to establish whether these particular new employees are sufficiently skilled for the work in hand and are generally acceptable to the rest of their current work teams.

If, following a limited period of employment, they are considered unsuitable, they are dismissed and others similarly employed, and this process continues until suitable employees are found. This approach puts most of the responsibility for selection with the first line supervisors and can present major problems regarding discrimination. It can also result in very varied selection policies and standards between different supervisors, which can lead to difficulties if it is ever necessary to transfer employees from one work team to another.

Modern employment legislation has tended to shift employment policies away from casual and easily abused systems, and many employers have now established formal procedures regarding the selection and appointment of employees. This means that first line supervisors, together with other employment specialists in the organization, may need to give careful consideration to:

SELECTION CONSIDERA-TIONS	• the criteria applicants should meet regarding the required levels of skill and experience
	• whether internal transfers are more appropriate than a new appointment
	• the appropriate job description and the terms and conditions of employment
	• the requirements of legislation regarding discrimination
	• whether it might be appropriate to employ disabled persons
	• whether applicants with previous employment experience with the organization should be given preference
	• whether there are any current agreements with trade unions or clients regarding employment policies
	• whether current application forms are suitable
	• whether interviews are appropriate and if so how and by whom will they be organized and what the applicants will be told about the job during their interviews.

The outcome of the recruitment and selection process is therefore the employment of persons who are, at that time, considered to be most likely to make positive contributions to the employer and who will be most effective in the work teams to which they are appointed.

THE INDUCTION OF NEW TEAM MEMBERS

Assuming the offer of employment has been accepted, it is important for the supervisor to establish the date and time at which the new employee will first be available for work. Many employers will require each new employee to complete standardized procedures on the first day of employment and before starting work. Often these procedures mean new employees are required to attend an office rather than a site at the start of their employment and to provide certain information, including:

STARTING WORK – THE BASIC DATA	• name and home address
	• National Insurance number
	• P45 tax certificate

- details of next of kin
- preferred arrangements for the direct credit of wages.

Once these administrative details have been completed, each new employee should be introduced to the appropriate supervisor or carefully briefed as to how to get to the site or how to find their appointed supervisor. The objective should be to minimize the time required to complete the initial employment administration efficiently, and to ensure that the supervisor and the new employee meet with the minimum of delay and confusion. Construction sites are not always easy to find, public transport may not be easy or particularly convenient and, unless the supervisor has been informed of the expected time of arrival of the new operative the supervisor may not be available when the employee arrives. If a new employee finds that it takes several hours of waiting around before making contact with the appropriate supervisor, the first impression may well be one of an inefficient and disorganized firm that does not place much value on its human resources.

The first few weeks of employment should be used as an induction period in which the employee finds out as much as possible of the normal working practices of the team and the employer; and the supervisor, on behalf of the team and the employer, considers how suitable the employee is for long term employment. The supervisor should therefore pay particular attention to the following:

| SUPERVISORY TASKS DURING THE INDUCTION PERIOD | • explaining procedures regarding:
  – time sheets
  – wages and bonus
  – pay arrangements
  – normal working hours and overtime opportunities
  – standards of behaviour and organizational rules about conduct
  – welfare facilities
  – safety arrangements and first aid
• explaining jobs and procedures in rather more detail than normal in order to reduce the opportunities for misunderstanding
• giving the new employee, as soon as possible, a task to do which does not involve other members of the team and which is well within the range of tasks an average employee with similar skills and experience is capable of completing satisfactorily, in order to make an initial assessment of the new employee's capability |

- arranging for the new employee to work on a range of tasks with other members of the team, so that all established team members have some experience of working with the new person
- selecting tasks in which the new employee can participate, and which are as representative as possible of the normal work of the team
- being available to the new employee rather more often than would normally be the case, in order to encourage questions and discussions about the work and the organization
- assessing the performance of the new employee fairly and to objective standards.

It is important that the supervisor uses this induction period to make a thorough assessment of the new employee's capabilities, skills and potential. With younger and less experienced employees more attention has to be paid to their potential, motivation and genuine interest in the work. With older and more experienced employees more attention can be paid to the existence of skills and demonstrations of abilities across a range of activities normally associated with the occupation.

IDENTIFYING STRENGTHS AND WEAKNESSES

It is also important to identify any serious problems or inadequacies the new employee may have regarding the work, to discuss these with the individual concerned and to suggest ways of overcoming any apparent difficulties. The supervisor will also want to talk with all the other members of the team to establish how well they feel the new employee is settling in, and to see if they have noticed particular strengths and weaknesses that should be considered during the induction period.

Supervisors should remember that the longer people remain in employment the more difficult it is to dismiss them for being incapable of doing the job properly. On the other hand dismissing someone for incompetence based on just a few hours of work might be a hasty decision which is both expensive for the employer and a permanent loss of someone with potential. It should usually be possible to make a fair assessment of a new employee's ability and potential at the end of the first month of employment and this should be considered a reasonable maximum for an induction programme for manual workers.

THE MOTIVATION OF THE TEAM AND ITS MEMBERS

In any group of workers in which all the members are performing similar tasks it will be noticed that some perform much better than others. It is now generally believed that there are two reasons for these differences in performance. One belief has been that such differences are related to the skill and experience of individual workers – that workers with more skill and experience perform better than those with less skill. This belief has encouraged some organizations to place greater emphasis on selection, on the design of tasks, on team building and on training. The second belief is that people vary in their willingness to direct their efforts towards meeting organizational objectives. Thus performance is dependent upon a **combination of ability and motivation**, and therefore it is necessary to consider what motivates workers to perform effectively.

APPROACHES TO MOTIVATION

During recent years three main approaches to motivation have been developed. The first of these has assumed that people will be motivated to perform their jobs more effectively if they are **satisfied with their employment**. Organizations which support this approach have good working conditions, clear promotion policies and may have pension schemes, recreation programmes and other fringe benefits, such as long service rewards, available to those who belong to the organization. The role of the first line supervisor in such organizations is therefore to help team members to feel comfortable and secure and to help them get what they want from the organization, and in return they will be loyal and highly motivated.

The second approach has been based upon the assumption that people will be motivated to work harder if **systems of rewards and penalties** are directly linked with performance. Organizations supporting this approach have bonus and profit sharing schemes, and promotion schemes based on merit. Such organizations also have systems of warnings, reprimands and sometimes dismissals, for those who break rules and procedures. The role of the first line supervisor here is therefore aimed at arranging work tasks so that team members have the best opportunities to earn bonuses, and at providing team members with early warning systems for inadequate performance.

The third approach to motivation has been based on what might be called **participative management**. This approach is based upon the assumption that individuals will obtain more satisfaction from completing tasks to which they are committed, and that commitment comes from their participation in the design of its working arrangements. Organizations supporting this approach may make arrangements for workers to participate in committees and study groups and may pay particular attention to suggestions which 'come up from the shop floor'. In such organizations the first line supervisor plays a helping or 'facilitating' function rather than having an authoritarian role, and is present as a resource for the team members to use.

However, few organizations select just one approach and many provide a wide range of opportunities for improving employee motivation. Sometimes these approaches may appear incompatible, as when employees are rewarded for long service and penalized for low output.

The supervisor therefore has a wide range of tasks that are associated with motivational issues. These include:

MOTIVATION – THE SUPER-VISORY TASKS	• knowing how the organization has approached motivation and performance issues and the organizational benefits, rewards, penalties and opportunities that exist for employee participation • knowing the interests and concerns of each member of the team • establishing ranges of satisfactory outputs associated with quality, quantity and the use of time, materials and equipment • discussing personal interests, commitment and concerns with individual members of the team • providing opportunities for employee participation, negotiation and discussion so that team members can become as fully involved as the organization allows • being available at crucial times for discussion and for solving unanticipated problems • objectively evaluating the performance of team members and discussing issues that arise • feeding back to higher management on the strengths and weaknesses of the organization's use of human resources.

THE CAREER DEVELOPMENT OF TEAM MEMBERS

Career development does not consist of simply providing team members with opportunities for promotion to supervisor. Not every employee wishes to be 'upwardly mobile'. Supervisors should be concerned with at least four main issues regarding career development.

First, there is the need to try and identify the personal interests of each team member. Some people will have no interest in promotion and will not want to be diverted from their current role. Others will be interested in moving to a new occupation or in gaining qualifications, and some will have plans to change their employment to a different industry. Consequently, it is not always easy to determine clear and precise career interests for all members of the team. Career interests change over time and personal circumstances can change very rapidly. Many employees are not prepared to discuss personal or family issues at work, so the supervisor has to be able to detect changes in attitudes and interests through general observations and day-to-day discussions, rather than through direct questions or interviews.

Secondly, the supervisor should provide opportunities for varied work experience for each member of the team. It is not always wise to restrict an employee to specific tasks just because it is convenient or because no-one else can do the job better. A varied set of work experiences can heighten interest, and limit boredom and rivalry between employees. Broadening the experiences of the team also minimizes problems when key team members are sick, on holiday or leave unexpectedly.

Thirdly, the supervisor should consider the opportunities which might arise to develop new skills within the team. These can arise because of changes in the nature of the work, opportunities to use new plant and equipment, and the advantage of having someone who can stand in for the supervisor during holiday periods. Different team members may have interests in different aspects of the work and this will assist the supervisor in forming proposals for skill development.

Fourthly, career development will often involve training. Supervisors should see that training opportunities are made known to all team members, and recommendations for attendance on courses should be based on a combination of organizational needs and personal interests. It is therefore important to recognize that the supervisor is an important link in career development strategies.

To provide an effective link the supervisor should know what opportunities exist within the organization, and see that these are brought to the attention of the team members. The supervisor should also have some ideas of the personal interests of all team members, and should be looking for ways in which these interests could be developed to the benefit of the individual, the team and the employer.

THE ROLE OF TRADE UNION REPRESENTATIVES

Employees need representatives to put forward their collective views to management and to safeguard their occupational interests. This function is best carried out by employees appointed as representatives of those independent trade unions which are recognized by the employer for the purposes of consultation, negotiation and collective bargaining. The functions of these trade union representatives should cover:

- **trade union matters** such as recruitment, maintaining membership and keeping members informed of trade union meetings and business
- **industrial relations matters** such as handling members' grievances, disputes and local negotiations and consultations.

The precise role of trade union representatives will vary according to the sector of industry in which the organization operates, and as a consequence of the industrial relations system which applies in that sector and in that specific organization.

Many supervisors see trade union representatives as problems to be avoided rather than as potential sources of assistance in developing more effective human resources at the work place. There are several aspects of the role of trade union representatives which supervisors should consider. These include:

TRADE UNION REPRESENTA-TIVES – SUPERVISORY CONSIDERA-TIONS	• establishing **the functions** of trade union representatives at the workplace; it is important that all the functions of these representatives should be clearly defined, and those relating to industrial relations should be agreed between the parties and recorded
	• agreeing on **the number** of trade union representatives to be appointed at the work place, and on the work groups for which each representative is responsible
	• agreeing on **the procedures** whereby trade union representatives are to be appointed and how elections are to be held
	• seeing that trade unions have given their representatives **written credentials**, setting out their powers and duties and stating the period of appointment and the work group to be represented
	• seeing that trade union representatives have the **facilities** to which they are entitled, and these should allow for them to have necessary time away from the job to attend to industrial relations affairs, provided permission has been obtained in advance from the appropriate supervisor; they are also entitled to the use of office facilities and access to a telephone
	• seeing that **management provides information** to trade union representatives on new employees, and on issues for which trade union involvement is required.

First line supervisors and trade union representatives should meet regularly to discuss issues of mutual interest and concern, including safety and employment procedures, and should meet as necessary to discuss the grievances of individual team members and collective disputes and disciplinary problems if and when these arise. It is absolutely essential that both trade union representatives and supervisors have copies of the current editions of any relevant

Working Rule Agreements, and that they have read and understood the rules that apply to the work in progress.

GRIEVANCE PROCEDURES

A grievance procedure is a method by which an individual or a small group of employees can raise queries or complaints about pay or working conditions. The aim of any such procedure should be to settle the grievance fairly and as closely as possible to the work place. The procedures should be simple and quick to operate. Grievance procedures should be in writing and:

GRIEVANCE PROCEDURES – THE KEY ISSUES	<ul><li>should normally allow for the grievance to be discussed in the first instance with the appropriate first line supervisor</li><li>if the first line supervisor cannot resolve the grievance without delay, the employee should be accompanied by the appropriate trade union representative, or by another employee, at subsequent discussions with higher management</li><li>should include a right of appeal</li><li>should provide for joint management and trade union committees to become involved if the grievance cannot be resolved by first line supervisors and managers</li><li>should also provide time limits for each stage of the procedure.</li></ul>

Thus it can be seen that first line supervisors and trade union representatives have opportunities to work together in the speedy identification and resolution of grievances.

DISPUTES PROCEDURES

Disputes may be related to the application or interpretation of existing contracts of employment or agreements between trade unions and employers, or they may relate to claims by employees or proposals by management for future terms and conditions of employment. Procedures for handling disputes should be in writing and should:

DISPUTES PROCEDURES – THE KEY ISSUES	<ul><li>state the level at which an issue should first be raised</li><li>state the stages which should follow if settlement cannot be agreed at the initial stage</li><li>lay down time limits for each stage of the procedure with provisions for extending these times by agreement</li></ul>

- not allow strikes, lock-outs or other forms of industrial action to take place until all stages of the
procedure have been completed and a failure to
agree formally recorded.

Legislation has necessitated regular changes in these written
procedures as governments have sought to reduce the damaging
effects of strikes. As a consequence, first line supervisors are usually
required to hand disputes over to the industrial relations specialists
within the organization.

DISCIPLINARY PROCEDURES

First line supervisors usually have a responsibility to operate
procedures that relate to the less serious instances of misconduct
that are performed by members of their teams. Many organizations
will have rules regarding serious misconduct, and will notify
employees of examples of behaviour which, if proved, would result in
instant dismissal. In all minor cases of misconduct it is necessary to
operate a **warning system**. This is to ensure that the employee
knows that repetitions of such conduct will be unacceptable, and will
result in disciplinary action which may eventually lead to dismissal.
Disciplinary procedures usually contain the following stages:

DISCIPLINARY
PROCEDURES
– THE KEY
ISSUES

- one or more **private oral warnings** of which
records should be kept by the supervisor
- a **final oral warning**, given in the presence of the
appropriate trade union representative or other
approved person, of which a record should be kept
and signed by the person receiving the warning
- a series of **written warnings** indicating the actions
which will be taken if the same pattern of behaviour
continues
- a **final written warning**
- an **investigation** of the situation and a recom-
mendation for appropriate action, which might
include dismissal
- an **appeal** procedure.

It is important for the supervisor to handle disciplinary matters
with care because they can so easily create poor working relationships between employees and employers if they are mishandled,
with the supervisor caught in the middle. They can also have
adverse effects upon the performance of the individuals concerned
and of the whole team. Therefore the ability of the supervisor to
create a team which performs to acceptable standards without the
use of grievance, disputes and disciplinary procedures is a clear
indication of the effective use of human resources.

SUMMARY

Craft supervisors need to pay careful attention to the effective use of human resources and this will involve, from time to time and with varying degrees of detail, choosing appropriate methods of recruitment and selection, the induction of new team members and the early identification of their strengths and weaknesses, the motivation of the team and its members, the career development of each member of the team and the effective use of trade union representatives in handling grievances, disputes and disciplinary procedures.

FURTHER STUDY OPPORTUNITIES

The following give a more detailed examination of the effective use of human resources:

BOASTON, I., CLEGG, H. and RIMMER, M., *Workplace and Union*, Heinemann 1975

HILTON, W. S., *Foes to Tyranny*, London, Amalgamated Society of Building Trade Workers 1963

HOBSBAWM, E. J., *Labouring Men*, Weidenfeld & Nicolson 1964

LITTLER, C. R., *The Experience of Work*, Gower 1985

MAIE, N. R. F., *The Appraisal Interview*, New York, John Wiley and Sons 1958

MCGREGOR, D., *The Human Side of Enterprise*, McGraw-Hill 1960

PRICE, R., *Masters, Unions and Men*, Cambridge University Press 1980

SIDNEY, E. and BROWN, M., *The Skills of Interviewing*, Tavistock Publications 1961

VROOM, V. H. and DECI, E. L., *Management and Motivation*, Penguin Books 1970

CHAPTER SEVEN

EMPLOYMENT ISSUES

This chapter examines seven broad areas in which first line supervisors should be both knowledgeable and careful regarding matters associated with employment. These include engagement, rights during employment, absence from work due to sickness, discrimination, trade union membership, procedures surrounding termination of employment, and issues associated with reclaiming equipment and protective clothing at the end of employment.

EMPLOYMENT LEGISLATION

Many employment issues in the United Kingdom are directly controlled by Acts of Parliament and indirectly influenced through membership of the European Community. There are many Acts of Parliament and other pieces of legislation which relate to employment, but because of the complexity, speed and frequency with which changes can be introduced into legislation, most employing organizations have staff with special responsibilities for employment matters, and for ensuring that employer and employees comply with statutory requirements. Therefore it is not usual for the first line supervisor to be directly responsible for matters associated with the engagement and termination of employment. However, the first line supervisor will often be one of the first persons an employee will approach about employment problems and therefore every supervisor must know the basic principles.

USING SPECIALIST PERSONNEL SERVICES

Supervisors must remember that they will be considered as part of the organization's management structure by employees. As a consequence employees will assume that advice given to them by their supervisor has the full support of the employer. Therefore it is important that supervisors use the specialist personnel skills available within the organization before taking action or giving advice. Wrong advice and actions by a supervisor can be expensive for the employer, embarrassing for the supervisor, and inconvenient and annoying for the employee as well as illegal. Errors, omissions and bad advice regarding employment issues are a major cause of poor working relationships between employees and their employers and supervisors.

ENGAGEMENT MATTERS

A person may be engaged either as an 'employee' or as a 'contractor'. Where the intention is to enter into 'an employer' and 'an employee' relationship this will take the form of a personal contract of employment. Where the intention is to enter into 'an employer' and 'a contractor' relationship this will take the form of a contract for services. The distinction between these two forms of legal relationship is important and must not be confused.

PART-TIME EMPLOYMENT

An employee may be engaged in part-time or in full-time employment. The rules for part time employment are complex and relate to the number of hours worked per week and to the length of continuous employment. Part-time employees usually do not have the right to a written statement of their terms of employment at engagement.

FULL-TIME EMPLOYMENT

Full-time employees may be engaged on a **fixed-term** or an **open-ended** contract of employment. A fixed-term contract must have a precise starting date and a precise termination date, and special considerations apply where fixed-term contracts are renewed without a break in employment.

WRITTEN STATEMENTS OF EMPLOYMENT TERMS

All full-time employees under either fixed-term or open-ended contracts are entitled to a written statement of the terms of their employment within 13 weeks of the start of their employment. This written statement should contain the following information:

WRITTEN
STATEMENTS
SHOULD
STATE . . .

- the date the statement is issued
- the name of the employer
- the name of the employee
- a broad general description of the job the employee is to do
- the date this employment began
- the date the employment is to end, if it is a fixed term contract
- the date any previous continuous employment began
- the rates of pay and when payments are to be made
- the normal working hours and the normal starting and finishing times of work
- entitlement to any holidays, holiday pay, sick-pay and pensions
- the notice that the employee has to give and the

> notice employees are entitled to receive from the employer
> - procedures for dealing with grievances
> - the disciplinary rules associated with the employment.

It is usual for these written statements to refer to other documents such as:
- pay-slips
- employment rules books.

It is also usual for written statements to refer employees to their supervisors for further information. Therefore it is important that all first line supervisors have an up-to-date copy of any employment rules book, and are carefully briefed regarding any changes to the statements given to individual employees.

The statement of employment terms is a statutory requirement. It is usual for all employees to be asked to sign that they have received a copy of the statement on a specific date. The statement of terms simply describes the terms of employment as seen by the employer and is therefore not a contract of employment.

WRITTEN CONTRACTS OF EMPLOYMENT

There is no statutory requirement to have a written contract of employment. However, many employers use written contracts of employment which incorporate the statement **of terms** and which encompass the whole of the working relationship between the employer and the employee. These written contracts are intended to be legally binding on both parties. Difficulties arise when some employment practices, such as overtime or revisions to the hours of work, are changed without revision being made to the contract documents. It is important that supervisors do not change the terms and conditions of employment of any employee, without first agreeing these with senior management and the employment specialists within the organization. Any changes in the terms and conditions of employment should be incorporated in a revised employment contract or statement of terms, and given to the appropriate employee within one month.

RIGHTS DURING EMPLOYMENT

The principal rights during employment relate to pay and the hours of work.

Pay

Pay is clearly one of the fundamental issues associated with employment. For some occupations there are nationally agreed rates of pay which are accepted by most employers. This applies particularly in the public sector. However, in many instances in the private sector, each employer is free to decide what the appropriate level of pay is for a particular job. At the more senior levels of appointment there are no minimum pay requirements or gradings that have to be observed, although some groups of employers may enter into arrangements between themselves that seek to limit salary differences for similar categories of jobs. Therefore, for many employees a rate of pay is offered by the employer and it is up to the individual employee whether to accept it or not. Consequently an employee's rights regarding pay during employment are very restricted. Equal treatment must be given to men and women in their terms and conditions of employment, and this implies that men and women employed on work similar in effort, skill or decision making should receive equal pay.

Normal hours of work

The statement of the terms of employment given following engagement should specify the normal hours of work if this is possible. This is important for at least two reasons. First, issues may arise during employment regarding 'overtime' and whether this is voluntary or not, and whether any overtime which is worked will be paid, and if so at what rate. Secondly, unless there is a clear statement of the hours at which employees are expected to be available for work, it is very difficult to discipline unauthorized absences from the work place without generating conflict.

Normal hours of work may present difficulties during periods when employees have to be laid off or kept on short time, or when there are guaranteed payments for specified workless days. There are also special rules regarding time off work for ante-natal care, and for employees with special public duty responsibilities. For those individuals who are officials of independent trade unions recognized by their employers, there is also a right to paid time off during working hours to carry out official duties. It is also important to specify the **holiday entitlement** of each employee and to state the periods of employment to which different holiday entitlements relate.

SICKNESS AND MEDICAL SUSPENSION

Employers are required to make a statutory sick payment to employees who are absent from work because of sickness and who qualify for sickness related payments. There are several factors that have to be taken into account regarding sick payments, including:

SICKNESS PROCEDURES – THE BASIC ISSUES	• ensuring that the employee concerned properly informs the employer when absence is due to sickness and that adequate evidence of sickness is provided

> - deciding on the appropriate period of incapacity from work
> - deciding which days of absence give an entitlement to statutory sick pay.

In most instances these are beyond the concern of first line supervisors. However, it is important that supervisors remind employees of the appropriate means of notifying their employer of absence for reasons of sickness.

Employees need to be reminded regularly of:

SICKNESS PROCEDURES – REMIND EMPLOYEES	<ul><li>whom they should contact in the event of absence through sickness</li><li>when and the form in which notification should be made</li><li>what evidence the employer will require regarding the nature of the sickness.</li></ul>

Supervisors should remember that special problems may relate to employees who live on their own, who have no established home address or who do not have English as their first language. In such instances supervisors should see that specialist personnel or wages staff are informed of all instances of unaccounted absence by employees which might have sickness or injury implications.

Very occasionally an employee may be suspended from work on medical grounds under the requirements of a specific Act of Parliament. In such instances the employee might be entitled to time off work with pay for a period of up to a maximum of 26 weeks.

DISCRIMINATION

It is illegal for any employer to discriminate against any employee on the grounds of **sex, race, colour, nationality or national or ethnic origins**. Discrimination can occur before employment starts, during or after employment has been terminated. It is unlawful for an employer to discriminate against a person during employment on the grounds of sex, either directly or indirectly, regarding opportunities for promotion, transfer or training or a wide range of other employment benefits. There is also a requirement that equal treatment is given regarding the terms and conditions of employment, and this includes pay and hours of work, where the work is of a broadly similar nature and where jobs have been given an equal value as a result of an evaluation study. There are some occasions when it may be allowable for an employer to differentiate on racial grounds, but this issue requires careful and specialist attention.

TRADE UNION MEMBERSHIP

The rights of those who are members of independent trade unions begin immediately they enter employment. There is no qualifying period. Similarly a person has the right not to belong to a trade union. Union members also have the right, if they give reasonable notice and subject to reasonable conditions, to terminate their membership of a union during a period of employment.

Employees sometimes find themselves in difficulties where, as operatives, they have been members of an appropriate occupational trade union recognized by their employer, and when promoted to supervisor status find that their employer recognizes another trade union for the purpose of **collective bargaining** with supervisory and managerial occupations. The decision to change membership from one recognized union to another can sometimes present supervisors with difficulties regarding their relationships with their previous work mates. This can be particularly difficult where the first line supervisor has been a union official in a craft union.

TERMINATION OF EMPLOYMENT

This issue presents most first line supervisors with difficulties at some time or other during their supervisory career. There are two areas which are of particular importance to supervisors, these concern **notice of termination** and **unfair dismissal**.

Notice of termination

Most employees have the right to certain **minimum periods of notice** where the employer intends to terminate employment. All employees have an obligation to give a minimim period of notice to their employer of their intention to terminate their employment. The contract of employment should state clearly the period of notice that an employee is entitled to receive and similarly, the contract should state the notice that an employee is expected to give to the employer. Supervisors must remember that although there are statutory minimum periods of notice, many employment contracts provide longer periods of notice than the statutory minimum. There are also many instances where notice periods have been negotiated between employers and recognized trade unions for groups of employees and these will often require specialist attention.

Notice is a statutory right and if an employer dismisses an employee without proper notice that is a breach of contract. It sometimes happens that the employer does not want to keep an employee at work during the notice period and **payment in lieu of notice** may be agreed with the employee concerned. In addition to the statutory right to notice, employees also have certain rights regarding payment during the period of notice. These rights to payment become complex where the employee is absent, or takes part in a strike during the period of notice.

It is therefore important that a supervisor should recognize the importance of clarifying the notice position, and this includes:

NOTICE – THE KEY ISSUES	• determining the appropriate notice period for each employee • establishing how notice of termination to be given • establishing whether the employee is expected to work through the period of notice, and if so what the normal hours of attendance will be • establishing whether the employee is not expected to work during the notice period, or is to have agreed periods of absence during that period.

It is also important to recognize that these issues should be clarified before an employee is given noticce, and that the supervisor knows to whom an employee should be referred in the case of uncertainties or problems regarding the period of notice.

Unfair dismissal

Employees with more than a specified minimum period of continuous full-time employment also have the statutory right **not to be unfairly dismissed**. In order to avoid unfairly dismissing an employee, an employer must have a reason for dismissal which falls within a number of specified categories. These categories are:

DISMISSAL – THE BASIC CATEGORIES	• capability or qualification • conduct • contravention of a duty, or restriction, imposed by an enactment • redundancy • some other substantial reason.

In each case it is necessary for the employer to justify the reason for terminating the employment. If the employer cannot prove that the dismissal was reasonable within the circumstances then the dismissal will be unfair. In two of these categories first line supervisors play a vital part.

It is important for the supervisor to recognize that these rights to protection against unfair dismissal do not apply from the start of employment, and that the supervisor plays an important part in ensuring that unfair dismissal does not occur.

With the category of **capability** the employer needs to show that the employee was incapable of doing the work because of inefficiency, sickness, injury, lack of appropriate qualifications, or because of some other incapacity. In the case of inefficiency it will be necessary for the employer to show that:

INEFFICIENCY – THE BASIC ISSUES	• the employee performed at an unacceptably low standard over a reasonably long period of time • the employer had tried to help the employee to

> improve performance through consultation and training opportunities
> - other more suitable employment, if available, had been offered to the employee.

Thus, the first line supervisor plays a vital role in determining unacceptable standards of performance, in bringing these to the attention of the employee and in suggesting ways in which the employee can improve. Finally the supervisor should maintain proper records so that should the employer eventually decide to terminate employment because of inefficiency, there is evidence of each instance of inefficiency. Where a first line supervisor is unconcerned with standards of performance it becomes increasingly difficult for the employer to prove inefficiency. This is because the employee can claim, with justification, that performance of this standard had been common for a long period of time and had never been questioned before.

With the category of **conduct**, proper procedures are even more important. In this category the employer is dismissing the employee for the offence of **misconduct**. In seeking to dismiss for misconduct the employer needs to establish that the offence was committed by the employee in question and that it was reasonable to dismiss the employee for that offence. Consequently many employers will not dismiss for misconduct without an investigation and an interview with the employee, and many employers will provide written guidance to all employees about:

MISCONDUCT
– GUIDANCE
NEEDED
GIVING . . .
- examples of gross misconduct for which it would be inappropriate to give warnings prior to considering dismissal
- examples of dismissals following warnings
- the disciplinary procedures to be followed by the employer when considering dismissal for misconduct.

The supervisor has an important role in determining unacceptable behaviour and in drawing this to the attention of employees. Many employers provide a written statement for all new employees of examples of the acts of gross misconduct for which dismissal would be considered without giving a prior warning. Such a statement will usually include reference to acts such as:

EXAMPLES OF
GROSS
MISCONDUCT
- theft or fraud
- dishonesty
- violent behaviour
- endangering the safety of other persons
- contravention of safety regulations

- wilful damage to company property
- offensive behaviour
- insubordination
- drunkenness
- drug abuse.

From time to time it may be appropriate for a supervisor to remind employees of the existence of such statements.

Most instances of misconduct at work are trivial rather than serious and consequently isolated instances should not lead directly to dismissal. In such cases it is normal for **a system of warnings** to operate. For at least the first instance of minor misconduct an oral warning should be given, for subsequent instances written warnings should be given. In most cases it will be the first line supervisor who is responsible for determining instances of misconduct and for implementing a system of oral warnings. The most obvious example of this is where an employee arrives at work late or is absent from the workplace during normal working hours without permission. In such cases it is important for the first line supervisor to warn the employee that such behaviour is unacceptable. If this is not done and a pattern of lateness and absence from the workplace is established without associated warnings, then the employee is entitled to claim that such behaviour is commonplace and the dismissal of one employee in such a situation would be unfair. Therefore first line supervisors must be alert to trivial misconduct and they must use the established disciplinary rules in the employer's interests.

Supervisors should establish with their work teams that the procedures regarding misconduct are generally understood. The following are the most important features to consider:

MISCONDUCT – THE BASIC ISSUES	• the rules for dealing with gross misconduct • the offences which should be warned in advance to allow the employer to consider the need for dismissal without further notice • the system of warnings to be given for trivial misconduct • the method to be used for giving warnings and for recording that warnings have been given and received by the employee • the procedures for investigating misconduct and for giving wayward employees the opportunity to justify their behaviour • the length of time warnings should remain on an individual's employment record • the length of notice to be given, or the pay to be given in lieu of notice, where a decision is made to dismiss an employee for misconduct

- whether a right of appeal is given to employees dismissed for misconduct, and if so how such appeals are to be held.

In the smaller organizations without specialists in personnel matters and industrial relations, first line supervisors must exercise great care in order to ensure that warnings and dismissals for misconduct are handled fairly and without discrimination.

Finally where dismissal is necessary for reasons of **redundancy**, there are detailed procedures which have to be followed regarding notification, union consultation, time off during the period of notice, and the nature of redundancy payments to be made. First line supervisors are not usually involved in such matters.

INDUSTRIAL TRIBUNALS

Where an employee complains to an industrial tribunal that dismissal was unfair or inappropriate, then it is possible for the tribunal to ask for a continuation of employment to be given or for the employee to be reinstated. For these reasons it is vital that supervisors handle the procedures associated with termination of employment fairly and without unpleasantness.

RECLAIMING EQUIPMENT AND PROTECTIVE CLOTHING AT THE END OF EMPLOYMENT

From time to time during the period of employment, employees may be allocated equipment and protective clothing for their personal use. In such cases it is important to clarify instances where the equipment is on *loan*, rather than a gift to the employee or a consumable item. The implication being that items which are on loan must be returned by the employee in reasonable condition at the end of the period of employment or when they are no longer required for the work in hand. In order to clarify this situation, employees should be required to sign a receipt for items on loan and a copy of these receipts should be kept on the employment record.

Once notice to terminate employment has been received, it often becomes the responsibility of the appropriate supervisor to ensure that any items on loan are returned in reasonable condition, and a receipt given to the employee recording that this has happened. Where the items are not returned by the required date or where they are returned in less than a satisfactory condition, then this must also be recorded. It is usually counter productive to try and claim payment from the employee for damaged or lost items.

SUMMARY

Legislation plays a major part in employment issues and consequently first line supervisors must liaise fully and carefully with the employment specialists within their organization. Supervisors must take care that all members of their team understand the principal terms and conditions of their employment.

Supervisors must ensure that they do not subject the members of their team to discrimination during employment.

The issues surrounding termination of employment should be of particular concern for first line supervisors, particularly the procedures associated with notice and unfair dismissal. Misconduct is a major issue for first line supervisors, especially those minor acts of misconduct for which dismissal is normally inappropriate.

FURTHER STUDY OPPORTUNITIES

The following give further information about employment matters, although care should be taken to ensure that any recent changes in legislation are always taken into account:

BUTLER, J. T., *Elements of Administration for Building Students*, Hutchinson, 3rd edition 1982

BURCH, T., *Absence Behaviour of Construction Workers*, Occasional Paper no 28, Chartered Institute of Building nd

PAYNE, D., *Employment Law Manual*, Gower Publishing Company. First published in 1975 and regularly updated by subscription

PAYNE, D. and MACKENZIE, K., *Employment Contract Manual*, Gower Publishing Company 1987

CHAPTER EIGHT

SAFETY ISSUES

This chapter will examine the need for safety policies and associated organizational arrangements, the sources of specialist help available to the first line supervisor, establishing safe methods of working, giving instructions and training for safe working procedures, workplace inspections and accident investigations.

LEGISLATION

Legislation has made health and safety precautions compulsory in places where construction works are carried out. Employers are generally responsible for the health and safety of their employees, and will need to consider the hazards associated with the work and the workplace, regardless as to who created these hazards. They must also assess the precautions that should be taken in order to protect employees against industrial injury and illness. The employer will also need to consider the safety of other persons associated with their work.

For instance, an employer whose employees erect a scaffold is responsible for seeing that it complies with the appropriate regulations when erected and available for use. An employer whose employees are to use that scaffold is responsible for seeing that it complies with the regulations whenever it is in use. Most of these issues are of direct concern to first line supervisors, who will usually be responsible for seeing that workplace health and safety precautions are properly implemented.

HEALTH AND SAFETY LEGISLATION

In 1974 the Health and Safety at Work etc Act became law. The main purpose of this act was to provide one comprehensive and integrated system of statutory law dealing with the health, safety and welfare of work people, and the health and safety of the general public affected by work activities. At the time the act was introduced it was described as the most significant statutory advance in the area of health and safety at work since the original Factory Act of 1833.

The 1974 Act contains enabling provisions which provide an 'umbrella' over other relevant Acts, such as The Factories Act 1961, and over a large number of subsidiary regulations such as The Construction (Working Places) Regulations 1966. The 1974 Act places general obligations on employers to protect their employees and others by the provision and proper maintenance of:

HEALTH AND SAFETY – THE EMPLOYER'S OBLIGATIONS	<ul><li>plant and systems of work that are safe</li><li>safe arrangements for the use, handling, storage and transport of articles and substances</li><li>sufficient information, instruction, training and supervision to enable all employees to avoid hazards and to contribute positively to their own safety and health at work</li><li>a safe and healthy place of work, and safe access to it and egress from it</li><li>a healthy working environment</li><li>adequate welfare facilities.</li></ul>

In addition each employer must prepare, revise as appropriate and make available to all employees, a **written statement of safety policy** and consult with safety representatives, as required by regulations.

However, first line supervisors cannot rest with the general provisions of the 1974 Act and need to use more detailed statutory provisions. These are arranged into four main groups:

HEALTH AND SAFETY REG-ULATIONS	<ul><li>**Regulations**, which include</li></ul> – The Construction (General Provision) Regulations, 1961
	    – The Construction (Lifting Operations) Regulations 1961
	    – The Construction (Working Places) Regulations, 1966
	    – The Construction (Health and Welfare) Regulations 1966
	    – The Woodworking Regulations 1974
	    – The Construction (Head Protection) Regulations 1990
	These, and other Regulations, state the precise statutory requirements for specified work activities and should be used by first line supervisors as reference documents.

HEALTH AND SAFETY PRESCRIBED NOTICES	<ul><li>**Prescribed Notices**, which include</li></ul> – Abstract of the Factories Act 1961 (Form F3)
	    – The Lead Paint Regulations 1927 (Form F996)
	    – The Abrasive Wheels Regulations 1970 (Form F2345).

These, and other Notices as appropriate, must be displayed, either on site, or in workshops, yards or offices attended by employees.

HEALTH AND SAFETY NOTIFICATIONS	• **Notifications to Factory Inspectors**, which include 　— Notice of Building Operations expected to last six weeks or more (form F10) 　— Notice of Accident or Dangerous Occurrence (Form 43B). These, and other Notifications, are required to be sent to specified persons when particular events occur. Usually Notifications will be sent from an organization's central office, but it is often wise for a first line supervisor to check that the appropriate actions have been taken.

HEALTH AND SAFETY PRESCRIBED REGISTERS	• **Prescribed Registers**, which include 　— General Register for Building Operations (Form 36) 　— Accident Book (Form BI 510A) 　— Records of Weekly Inspections, Examinations, Tests, etc (Form F91) 　— Register for the purposes of the Abrasive Wheels Regulations (Form F2346). These, and other appropriate Registers, are required to be kept on site or in the relevant offices and are to be completed by the appropriate persons at specified times or after specified events.

KEEPING THE SUPERVISOR INFORMED

The first line supervisor should be informed by the employer or a senior manager, of the statutory provisions which apply to the work in hand, should receive copies of the appropriate documents and should be informed of the statutory records that need to be completed as the work proceeds.

POLICY STATEMENTS AND ORGANIZATIONAL ARRANGEMENTS

The 1974 Health and Safety at Work Act requires employers, except in prescribed cases, to '. . . prepare and as often as may be appropriate revise a written statement of his general policy with respect to the health and safety at work of his employees and the organisation and arrangements for the time being in force for carrying out that policy, and to bring the statement and any revision of it to the notice of all of his employees'.

A great deal of freedom has been given to employers to provide safety policy statements which reflect their own areas of activities and organizational structure. However, the following issues should be considered in the preparation of an effective organizational policy for safety and health:

SAFETY POLICY STATEMENTS SHOULD COVER . . .	• the organization's basic objectives and supplementary detailed rules and procedures which cater for specific hazards associated with the work
	• the definition of the duties and the extent of the responsibilities at specified levels of line management and supervision, and the identification of the person at the highest level within the organization who has overall responsibility for health and safety matters
	• the definition of the functions of safety officers and specified safety supervisors and their relationship to line management and supervision
	• the procedures installed for monitoring safety performance and for publishing information about that performance
	• the procedures for regularly identifying hazards associated with the work of the organization
	• a description of the information system installed for keeping employees at all levels informed of the effectiveness of the policy and associated organizational arrangements
	• a description of the safety training provisions available to all levels of employees within the organization
	• the provisions for consultation with trade unions regarding matters of safety and for worker participation in safety arrangements.

Such a statement is insufficient in itself and it will be necessary for each employer to demonstrate the arrangements currently in force:

SAFETY – THE DYNAMIC ARRANGE-MENTS	• for allocating safety responsibilities among managers, supervisors and safety officers and for assessing their effectiveness
	• for identifying and controlling safety hazards, particularly those associated with plant and machinery
	• for identifying and controlling health hazards, particularly those associated with noise, toxic and corrosive substances and dust

> - for site inspections, safe operating procedures, accident investigations and safety audits
> - for safety training.

Therefore an effective safety system has a **statement of general policy**, supported by a **set of dynamic arrangements**, for regularly monitoring performance and for minimizing hazards to health and safety at work.

SOURCES OF SPECIALIZED HELP AVAILABLE TO SUPERVISORS

In many organizations the nature of the work is sufficiently varied, specialized or hazardous that it would be unreasonable to expect line managers to be capable of identifying all the likely hazards, determining all the appropriate procedures and making all the appropriate tests and inspections. Therefore it is normal for many organizations to appoint specialists to assist line managers in health and safety matters.

The following persons may have special safety responsibilities:

PEOPLE WITH SPECIAL RESPONSIBILITIES FOR SAFETY	<ul><li>specialists responsible for the design of equipment, false work, and methods of work may be required to carry out tests on their designs before they are used, and to provide line management and first line supervisors with adequate information on how the equipment and methods of work should be used safely</li><li>specialists responsible for the purchase of plant, equipment and materials may be required to provide line management with adequate information on safe methods of installation, handling, storage and use</li><li>those responsible for the maintenance of mechanical plant and equipment may be required to carry out periodic tests and inspections, will almost certainly be required to look for signs of improper use, and may be required to provide line management and first line supervisors with appropriate reports</li><li>where fire officers are appointed, they will be required to make appropriate inspections and tests and to report to line management as necessary</li><li>where safety officers and safety supervisors are appointed they will have defined duties and responsibilities.</li></ul>

In each of these cases first line supervisors should know who the specialists are within their organization, and should be given clear guidance on their specialist skills and how these skills can be made available to them. This requires senior management to provide a considered and proper delegation of specialized health and safety responsibilities to persons with specialist skills, qualifications, experience and equipment. These specialists may be full-time employees within the organization, they may be specialist consultants who are available only at specified times or they may be specialist contractors. First line supervisors therefore need to know what specialist health and safety services are available and how these might be contacted if needed.

ESTABLISHING SAFE METHODS OF WORKING

Safe systems of work should be established for all high risk activities and for activities which are infrequently performed, instances where the work is being undertaken in close proximity to other employees or members of the public, or where the work is being carried out in occupied buildings. First line supervisors should also consider the need for safe systems of work for employees who are particularly vulnerable; including trainees, newly appointed operatives, young people and the elderly or disabled.

It is not necessary to design a safe method of work for each and every building operation. Tasks which are common to a particular occupation and which are being undertaken regularly by qualified and experienced employees with readily available, adequate and proper equipment, should be undertaken safely without specialist instructions from the supervisor. Of course, in such situations, first line supervisors should provide a reasonable level of supervision as the work proceeds. However, there will be some tasks on many projects which have unique features, or which involve the use of new materials or equipment.

A supervisor should consider the answers to the following questions when in doubt about the necessity to provide an employee with a safe system of work:

SAFE SYSTEMS OF WORK – ARE THEY NEEDED?	• does the employee know the hazards associated with the work? • does the employee know the precautions which should be taken against such dangers? • are the necessary precautions readily available? • does the employee know that the precautions are available? • has the employee been trained in the proper use of the precautions?

Providing answers to these questions requires the supervisor to think about the nature of the task, the appropriate precautions and their availability, and the selection and briefing of the employee who will do the work. Thus the supervisor needs to think ahead. There may be many situations when no member of the team has any previous experience of the work, materials or equipment in question and in such cases specialist help should be obtained before work starts.

Safe methods of working need not involve elaborate instructions. It may be sufficient for the supervisor to demonstrate the task to the operative and to supplement the demonstration with a simple checklist.

GIVING INSTRUCTIONS AND TRAINING FOR SAFE WORKING PROCEDURES

The Health and Safety at Work Act imposes a clear obligation on all employers to provide '... such information, instruction, training and supervision as is necessary to ensure as far as is reasonably practicable, the health and safety at work of his employees'. Instruction and training needs can be considered under four main headings:

INSTRUC- TIONS AND TRAINING MAY BE NEEDED RE- GARDING . . .	• legal requirements • hazards at work • safe working methods . • accident prevention.

Much instruction and training can be given at the workplace by the first line supervisor as part of the normal supervisory activities. This will be particularly straightforward on projects that are well within the normal range of the organization's work. Clearly, there are four areas in which special instructions and training might be appropriate. These include provisions for **new employees**, particularly **hazardous activities, tasks and equipment new** to the organization, and **training for first line supervisors**. Such specialist training should be provided by the employer, either directly through internal safety courses, or indirectly by using external training facilities.

WORKPLACE INSPECTIONS

The main reason for having systems of workplace inspections is to attempt to identify potential hazards so that action can be taken to control or eliminate them and thus prevent accidents occurring. Inspections may be undertaken independently by supervisors, by safety specialists, by trade union safety representatives, or there may be joint inspections. There are several reasons why joint inspections are advisable, these include:

JOINT WORKPLACE INSPECTION	• promoting joint understanding of health and safety problems • encouraging collaboration between specialists in order to control or eliminate hazards • developing cooperation between management, employees and trade unions regarding health and safety matters.

Workplace inspections should be undertaken:

WORKPLACE INSPECTIONS ARE NEEDED	• on a regular basis to monitor safety standards and to identify potential hazards • after significant changes in plant, equipment or workplace layout • following the publication of guidance on hazard identification relevant to the workplace • following accidents, notifiable diseases and dangerous occurrences.

There are several types of workplace inspection, of which the most common are:

WORKPLACE INSPECTIONS – BASIC TYPES	• **safety audits**, in which each area of an organization's activity is subjected to systematic examination, including safety policy, workplace layout, operating procedures, training and attitudes and aims to identify the strengths and weaknesses and the main hazards and areas of risk • **safety inspections**, in which routine scheduled inspections are made of a site, workshop or department, and these inspections would check the extent to which work was being carried out in accordance with procedures, working practices, maintenance standards and the extent of employee involvement • **safety tours**, in which unscheduled examinations are made of a work area in order to observe general safety standards, to determine whether standards of housekeeping are being maintained at a satisfactory level, and to see that obvious hazards are identified and removed.

With all workplace inspections, first line supervisors must be fully informed of organizational policies and procedures, properly trained in the appropriate inspection techniques, fully involved in the discussion of inspection results and in the implementation of subsequent improvements.

ACCIDENT INVESTIGATIONS

An accident is any unplanned, unwanted event which may or may not lead to injury, illness, loss or damage. Therefore accident investigations must not be restricted to instances where there have been serious personal injury. An accident cause is an uncontrolled hazard without which there could be no accident. Therefore accidents may be caused by any combination of plant, equipment, premises, materials, environment, systems of work and people.

Accident investigations should aim primarily to prevent a similar event ever occurring again, a secondary aim may be to identify who was responsible for the accident and whether any disciplinary or legal action should be taken because of negligence. Many organizations have established accident investigation procedures and these are often applied by people with no line management responsibilities for the work. The following set of questions could be used to form the basis of an accident investigation:

ACCIDENT INVESTIGATIONS – SOME BASIC QUESTIONS	<ul><li>was the person concerned carrying out a task that was part of this person's normal duties?</li><li>was the task within the job description of the person concerned?</li><li>was the person involved in an activity which was associated with work but was not directly related to a task?</li><li>was the person's first line supervisor present in the area at the time of the accident?</li><li>was a report of the accident prepared without delay?</li><li>who prepared the accident report?</li><li>what warnings of the hazards associated with the task had been given to the person when the task was allocated?</li><li>what instructions were given to the person regarding the method of undertaking the task?</li><li>was the work carried out in accordance with written instructions or the normal custom and practice of the workplace?</li><li>was the task within the normal capabilities of the person concerned?</li><li>was the person concerned familiar with the type of plant, equipment or tools used for the task?</li><li>what training had the person received to carry out this task?</li><li>what protective clothing was worn by the person concerned at the time of the accident?</li><li>was the clothing worn and equipment used adequate protection against the hazard?</li></ul>

- was the plant and equipment in proper working condition at the time of the accident?
- were guards and other protective devices on plant and equipment effective and secure?
- were there any emergency stop provisions on the plant, and if so were these close at hand?
- were the statutory warning notices displayed appropriate for the equipment in use?
- were operating controls clearly marked?
- was there any obstruction in the access to and egress from the workplace?
- were there any failures of services, components, plant or equipment at the time of the accident?
- what procedures are there for monitoring systems of work?
- what procedures are there for workplace inspections and for warning employees of the hazards associated with their work?
- are permits to work normally issued for this kind of work?
- was a permit to work issued to the person concerned with this task?
- were the conditions of the permit being followed at the time of the accident?

As can be seen many of these issues may directly or indirectly involve the first line supervisor. For this reason it is normal for first line supervisors to be excluded from accident investigations. Of course the line managers and supervisors will be required to answer many of the questions raised during the investigation. Therefore it is important that all supervisors maintain proper records of the instructions, demonstrations and training given to their team members and of the workplace inspections made.

Where there has been serious personal injury or other notifiable occurrence, it will be necessary for the accident to be reported to the proper authorities and for appropriate investigations to be made by government inspectors. Where these investigations reveal that there has been a contravention of the statutory requirements by the employer, then legal action will be taken. Remember that **the construction industry has one of the worst accident records in the whole of British industry**, and the courts have little sympathy for employers, managers or supervisors who blatantly ignore the statutory requirements for health and safety at work.

SUMMARY
Legislation has now provided for one comprehensive and integrated system of statutory law dealing with health and safety at work

which should be of concern to employers, supervisors, trade unionists and employees. Employers should keep their supervisors informed of the statutory provisions which apply to the work in hand and should see that all supervisors know of the internal arrangements which have been provided in order to comply with statutory requirements.

Safe systems of work should be established for all high risk activities and for employees who may be particularly vulnerable to accidents. Supervisors should consider what work place based training is necessary to minimize the possibility of accidents, and regular workplace inspections should be undertaken to identify potential hazards.

When accidents occur there should be thorough and impartial investigations aimed at preventing similar accidents occurring again.

FURTHER STUDY OPPORTUNITIES

The following give further explanation of the safety issues associated with construction work, however it is important to keep abreast of new legislation.

ARMSTRONG, P. T., *Fundamentals of Construction Safety*, Hutchinson 1980

BUILDING EMPLOYERS CONFEDERATION, *Construction Safety*, BEC, updated manual

HEALTH AND SAFETY EXECUTIVE, *Effective Policies for Health and Safety*, HMSO 1980

HEALTH AND SAFETY EXECUTIVE, *Guidance of Health and Safety Advisory Services for the Construction Industry*. Part 1: The need for advice and the services available. Part 2: The safety adviser: selection, training and professional standards, HMSO 1983

HEALTH AND SAFETY EXECUTIVE, *Managing Health and Safety in Construction: Principles and Application to Main Contractor/Sub Contractor Projects*, HMSO 1987

HEALTH AND SAFETY EXECUTIVE, *Safety Representatives and Safety Committees*, HMSO 1988

LANEY, J. C., *Site Safety*, London, Construction Press 1982

CHAPTER NINE

RESOURCES – MATERIALS, PLANT AND EQUIPMENT

This chapter considers some of the main responsibilities of first line supervisors for calculating the quantities of materials required, for making allowances for waste, and for operating within the organization to requisition, call forward, receive and despatch materials, plant and equipment. This chapter also considers issues associated with unloading, inspecting and storage at or near the workplace, for the proper economic use of materials, plant and equipment and for the care and maintenance of plant and equipment.

RESPONSIBILITIES FOR MATERIALS, PLANT AND EQUIPMENT

Most construction tasks require materials, plant or equipment in addition to human resources. Therefore first line supervisors will often need to consider the specific materials, plant and equipment requirements for each task their teams undertake. However, in most organizations there are departments with special responsibilities for the purchasing or procurement of materials and for the management of plant and equipment. Consequently, most first line supervisors will need to collaborate with these specialist departments in order to make the most efficient use of the plant and materials that might be available to them.

CALCULATING QUANTITIES OF MATERIALS

First line supervisors may be required to assist those with specialist responsibilities for the procurement of materials and plant by providing specific project information and by checking the quantities of materials required. The contract or order documents will contain information about the materials to be used on any specific project. These contract documents are often complex and numerous and may include, among other things, drawings, specifications, bills of quantities, schedules, and written instructions issued as the work has proceeded. The first line supervisor must know which documents are the contract documents and which other documents have been issued under the authority of the contract documents. In many instances first line supervisors will need to take advice from senior line management within their organization regarding the contract documents for each project.

STUDYING THE CONTRACT DOCUMENTS

Having established the precise contract documents, these must be studied carefully in order to identify all the information and dimensions that relate to each specific item of work, material or component. Sometimes the information given on one document, such as a drawing, will conflict with the information given on another document, and the supervisor must seek guidance from line management regarding any such discrepancies. Supervisors must never make assumptions about the relative importance of different contract documents.

TAKING SITE DIMENSIONS

Having established the contract requirements for the materials or components required, it will normally be necessary to take site dimensions. These become increasingly important as the work on site proceeds. In many instances the supervisor will find it helpful to produce a schedule of the materials or components required. In this way the materials or components can be scheduled for each room, elevation or building. It will also be important for the supervisor to consider the degree of accuracy required when taking site dimensions, and the equipment necessary to work within the required accuracy or manufacturing tolerance. Where the quantities involved are extensive the supervisor is wise to have someone check the calculations in order to minimize the chances of error.

USING MANUFACTURERS' CATALOGUES

With many components, such as ironmongery, drainage goods or special bricks a copy of the manufacturer's catalogue will be required. Where the contract documents specify the manufacturer or the product range, it is a relatively simple matter to obtain the necessary catalogues. Where the manufacturer is not stated, it will be necessary to establish with the buying department the form in which schedules of materials should be produced for tendering purposes. In some of the larger organizations schedules are produced by specialists for the first line supervisor to check. These checks must be made carefully, and discrepancies, errors or uncertainties identified by the supervisor and notified to the buyer without delay. Copies of the appropriate manufacturer's documentation will be needed for this purpose.

CHECKING SUB-CONTRACTORS' AND SUPPLIERS' DRAWINGS AND SCHEDULES

In some instances, sub-contractors and suppliers will be required to visit the workplace to take dimensions for components to be manufactured off site, and often they will send drawings or schedules, following such visits, to the site asking for them to be checked. First line supervisors should seek the advice of their line managers before complying with such requests, because the consequences of undetected errors may have contractual implications.

MAKING ALLOWANCES FOR WASTAGE

With many materials and components, but by no means all, some allowance must be made for waste. This is because it may not be possible to use in the work all the items ordered or delivered. Obvious examples of where some waste is normal include facing bricks, carcassing timber, nails, drainage goods and plasterboard. Examples of where it is unusual to make any allowance for wastage include components such as doors, windows, baths, and ironmongery.

First line supervisors will need to consider the appropriate wastage allowances to be made for each material and component to be ordered. This is by no means a simple matter, as there are several issues to be considered. First, many manufacturers may find it easier and cheaper for them to supply materials, and sometimes components, that are in excess of the quantities ordered. Secondly, suppliers may only be prepared to deliver in minimum quantities. Thirdly, the design of the component or work may not take into account the normal market sizes of materials or the manufactured sizes of components, and cutting to waste might be cheaper than ordering specialist sizes or components. Finally, the labour costs involved in avoiding waste may be more than the cost of additional materials.

The first line supervisor will need to assess whether any allowances should be made regarding the amount of waste to be included in any order or requisition. Several factors should influence this decision, including:

ALLOWANCE FOR WASTE – BASIC CONSIDERATIONS	<ul><li>the possibility of obtaining identical materials, perhaps from the same batch, if insufficient materials are ordered initially and an additional order has to be placed</li><li>the minimum size of orders which can be placed without incurring additional delivery costs</li><li>the cost of the delays which may occur if the materials are used up before the work is completed</li><li>whether the delivery of the materials should be phased so that wastage levels can be monitored as the work proceeds</li><li>whether the site conditions are so cramped that delivery in small quantities is essential</li><li>whether purchasing larger quantities than required for a specific task has discount implications and the surplus materials can be used on other projects</li></ul>

> - whether the cost of the additional handling and clearance of surplus materials and their storage until eventual use is justified.

Once these issues have been considered the supervisor is in a position to determine the appropriate amount of waste to be included in the order or requisition. This figure should be recorded and used to control the wastage levels during the progress of the work.

CONTROLLING WASTAGE LEVELS

When seeking to control the level of waste occurring on a project, the supervisor will need to consider three factors:

CONTROLLING WASTE – BASIC CONSIDERATIONS	- the materials to be charged to the project might already include an element of waste, or might have been bought very cheaply because some cutting to waste was foreseen - some materials which have become unsuitable for their intended purpose might be used for some other legitimate purpose, for instance where chipped facing bricks can be used as common backing bricks - the ease with which some materials which might get lost or otherwise unaccounted for during the construction process.

When controlling waste, first line supervisors should compare the quantities of materials delivered with the remaining stock and the amount of work satisfactorily completed. So, in a very simple example, if 10,000 facing bricks have been delivered, and there are remaining stocks of 2,000 bricks and the finished work accounts for 7,500 bricks then 5% of the delivered facing bricks are unaccounted for and should be investigated. If an original wastage level of 5% was included in the order then there should be enough facing bricks to finish the work, and a quick check will inform the supervisor if the outstanding work will require not more than 1,900 facing bricks. Checks like this should be made at either monthly intervals, if the projects have reasonably long time scales, or at stages when (say) 25%, 50% and 75% of the work is complete. These regular checks allow the supervisor to use the data collected to reduce the wastage levels for future requisitions, or to increase the level of supervision.

REQUISITIONING OR CALLING FORWARD MATERIALS, PLANT AND EQUIPMENT

In most cases formal orders for the purchase of materials and components, or for the purchase or hire of plant and equipment, will be placed centrally. In some organizations supervisors will be required to make initial requisitions so that these orders can be placed and in other organizations the orders will be placed centrally and, after the orders have been placed, the first line supervisors will be required to call forward materials, plant and equipment for delivery, as and when required, within the general terms of the initial order.

REQUISITIONING PLANT AND MATERIALS

There are a number of issues that require the careful consideration of first line supervisors regarding requisitions for plant and materials. These include:

PLANT AND MATERIALS REQUISITIONS – SOME BASIC ISSUES	• establishing that the first line supervisor has **the necessary authority**, and is required to requisition the materials or plant; problems can arise when no-one initiates the procurement system or when the same materials are requisitioned in different ways and at different times by different people
	• establishing the **precise descriptions** of the materials, plant or equipment required; this includes an examination of the appropriate clauses in contract documents and seeing that all the appropriate tools and accessories are ordered with main items of plant and equipment
	• seeing that the **correct quantities**, with proper allowance for waste, have been calculated and included as appropriate on lists or schedules
	• establishing whether the materials or equipment are to be **delivered or collected**
	• seeing that the correct full **postal address** has been given for delivery; where the deliveries have to be made to a specific entrance to a site, building or works then full details must always be given
	• seeing that all special instructions regarding **delivery arrangements** are included, these might include the date and times when deliveries can be accepted, the maximum size of lorry that can gain access to the works or site, unloading arrangements, including giving the name of the person responsible for accepting goods at the work place
	• where mechanical plant is being requisitioned, it will be necessary to state if a **driver or operator** is required and if special attachments or tools are required
	• where more than one delivery will be necessary to complete the order, whether the materials, compo-

nents, plant or equipment should be delivered in any particular **sequence or rate of delivery**

- where mechanical plant and equipment is being requisitioned, the period during which the plant is required on site should be stated; where continuous use of mechanical plant cannot be maintained throughout the period, this should be stated and the **non working periods** stated on the requisition
- where there are **minimum delivery periods** the supervisor will need to ensure that requisitions are sent to the appropriate departments in time for the orders to be processed so that the deliveries can be made on time – in some instances supervisors will have to requisition materials many weeks before they are required on site
- all requisitions should be **dated and authorized** by the appropriate person
- the supervisor should keep a **copy of all the requisitions raised** and should file them together with copy orders and call forward notices.

AVOIDING MISTAKES

Requisitions therefore take time to produce and check. Mistakes can easily occur if they are produced in a hurry, without carefully checking the contract documents, and without taking necessary site dimensions and getting someone else to check the calculations if these are complex.

COPY ORDERS

Once the requisition has been received by the appropriate central department and any queries resolved, a formal order will be placed and at least one copy of each order should be sent to the first line supervisor concerned. All these copy orders must be carefully checked as soon as they are received and the appropriate department contacted without delay if there are any errors, discrepancies or items that are unclear. On large projects, where there are many orders to place, great care is needed at this checking stage, because:

CHECK THE COPY ORDERS BECAUSE . . .	<ul><li>there may have been changes to the contract requirements and sometimes details of these changes do not reach the procurement departments before orders are generated</li><li>checking the order provides the supervisor with an opportunity to consider the unloading and storage arrangements and to check that the order gives all the appropriate details</li></ul>

- the formal order provides the supervisor with an opportunity to contact the supplier and check that all the details on the order are understood and to ask for details of appropriate unloading and storage requirements.

PARTIAL DELIVERY ARRANGEMENTS

It may be necessary to discuss with the supplier the arrangements to be made for calling forward deliveries when the whole order cannot be delivered or received at once. First line supervisors should appreciate that suppliers will normally wish to deliver the whole order as quickly as possible, particularly when they can deliver from stock and want to reduce their stocks or increase their sales figures. Alternatively manufacturers may want to arrange their partial deliveries of a large order to suit their own manufacturing or transport arrangements. However, the first line supervisor may not have the storage space or facilities to accept the whole delivery at once, and the employer may wish to spread the payments over a relatively long period. Therefore partial delivery arrangements require careful negotiation.

RECEIVING DELIVERY AND UNLOADING MATERIALS AT THE WORKPLACE

Whenever possible deliveries should be planned in advance so that the first line supervisor has time to arrange for the proper inspection of the goods on arrival, and for appropriate unloading and storage facilities to be made ready. Where the orders are for complex, easily damaged or expensive goods, and the manufacturer is within a reasonable distance of the workplace, much benefit can be gained by inspecting the works during the manufacturing period. It is, however, usual for the first line supervisor's first sight of the materials to be when they arrive at the workplace on the delivery vehicle. Even this can present problems when the materials are packaged in such a way that they cannot be easily checked.

MAKING PROPER INSPECTIONS

Once the delivery vehicle arrives the supervisor has a number of crucial actions to undertake before unloading starts. These include:

CHECKING
DELIVERIES
- checking that the materials or plant and equipment have been delivered to the correct site
- checking that the details on the delivery ticket correspond to those on the original order, this is sometimes difficult and time consuming
- checking that the goods have been packaged as stated on the order form and that appropriate and safe means of unloading are available

- checking that there are no obvious signs of physical damage to the materials
- establishing that the vehicle can be driven to the place where unloading is to take place and that unloading can be completed within the agreed time.

UNLOADING

Once these preliminaries have been completed unloading can start. The first line supervisor should consider the following aspects of unloading, whether:

UNLOADING – THE BASIC ISSUES

- the people involved in the unloading process are properly trained for the work and are being properly supervised
- the unloading process is being undertaken safely and is in accordance with the manufacturer's or supplier's instructions
- the materials can be properly checked for physical damage during the process of unloading
- any simple tests or checks should be undertaken during unloading
- any certification has to be provided with the delivery note confirming that the goods comply with appropriate and agreed tests or inspection requirements.

SIGNING DELIVERY TICKETS

If the above factors have been given proper consideration, then the first line supervisor should be in a position to sign the delivery ticket once the unloading is complete. Any discrepancies should be recorded on the delivery ticket and if these are considerable, then senior line management should be advised and guidance sought before signing the delivery ticket. One copy of the delivery ticket should be retained by the supervisor, and once the delivery has been recorded on any materials schedule in use, the delivery note should be forwarded to the appropriate department.

First line supervisors should remember that discounts may be available if the accounts are settled within a specified period, therefore the transmission of delivery notes should not be delayed. There might also be situations where pallets or packing cases are charged for or where additional charges are made if unloading takes longer than a specified period. Care should be taken to ensure that the need for any such additional charges has been agreed and recorded on the job ticket.

MAKING STORAGE ARRANGEMENTS FOR MATERIALS, PLANT AND EQUIPMENT

Shop based supervisors have few opportunities to design new storage layouts for materials or plant, but on site there are many opportunities for the first line supervisor to consider storage arrangements. Where space on site is restricted or where the scene of the work frequently changes from one place to another, making effective storage arrangements can be problematic, and a balance of some kind has to be struck between frequent movement of stores and compounds, and poor access arrangments. Therefore first line supervisors should evaluate their storage arrangements regularly and the following are some of the issues that should be considered:

STORAGE ARRANGEMENTS – THE BASIC ISSUES	• the convenience of the store for purposes of unloading • size of the storage area for the quantity of materials, plant or equipment to be stored • ease of handling and use from storage positions • security against theft • protection against damage • protection against weather • whether it is possible to comply with the manufacturer's or supplier's recommendations for storage • minimum inconvenience to others • minimum safety or health hazards.

On projects with very limited space, or where work has to be undertaken in occupied buildings much thought will be required regarding storage arrangements. On some very restricted sites it may be necessary to arrange off site storage facilities and these arrangements present major problems for first line supervisors, who then need to spend much more time and effort in carefully scheduling their materials for delivery when required.

MAKING EFFECTIVE USE OF MATERIALS, PLANT AND EQUIPMENT AT THE WORKPLACE

There are some obvious arrangements that supervisors can make, and these include:

EFFECTIVE USE OF RESOURCES – SOME BASIC ISSUES	• keeping expensive and fragile materials in secure storage areas • keeping powered hand tools and leads locked up when not in use • allocating just sufficient materials, including an adequate allowance for waste, to each operative for each job

- regularly checking powered hand tools and equipment for safety and for signs of excessive wear or misuse
- checking that wastage levels do not become excessive
- keeping the workplace tidy and collecting off cuts and surplus materials for future use
- arranging for regular safety checks of the workplace and the plant and equipment in use, involving the team members in debriefing sessions following these inspections
- providing regular training and demonstrations in the most effective use of plant and equipment, this could take just a few moments each week.

The aims should be for the first line supervisor to:

EFFECTIVE USE OF MATERIALS – THE SUPERVISORY ISSUES	- be constantly on the look out for signs of waste and inefficiency - limit opportunities for abuse of tools and materials by restricting unauthorized access to expensive materials and plant - encourage and reward safe practice - use the special skills within the organization to provide an external system of inspection and supplementary support to the supervisor as the work proceeds.

DESPATCHING SURPLUS MATERIALS, PLANT AND EQUIPMENT FROM THE WORKPLACE

Generally speaking surplus plant, equipment and materials should be moved from the workplace as soon as possible. There are several reasons for this, including:

DEALING WITH SURPLUS MATERIALS AND PLANT – SOME BASIC ISSUES	- the reduction of hire charges - freeing up space on site for other purposes - preventing the unnecessary deterioration of materials - minimizing safety and health hazards on site - reducing opportunities for pilfering and deliberate damage.

The despatch of surplus equipment has to be carefully arranged, if it is not then problems will arise. First line supervisors should consider the following questions when arranging for surplus items to be despatched from the workplace:

DISPATCH ARRANGE- MENTS – SOME BASIC ISSUES	<ul><li>have all the surplus items been identified and listed, together with any reference numbers, so that nothing is left behind?</li><li>are all the items in good order, if not will damaged items need to be listed separately, and marked so that they are not used before repair and testing?</li><li>what size vehicle will be required and what special loading and unloading arrangements are necessary?</li><li>when the items will be ready for collection, where they are located and who is to be contacted on arrival regarding loading arrangements?</li><li>whether directions are necessary to find the site or workplace?</li></ul>

Plant managers and hire companies may not want to collect surplus plant too quickly, they may have no other project requiring that equipment, they may not have transport readily available or they may have another site in the vicinity which is not yet ready for them. Consequently, they may prefer to leave the plant and equipment on site to be collected at some later date. In such cases it is essential for the first line supervisor to ensure that the plant is taken off hire, that it is made safe and where its continued presence on site is inconvenient, higher management is informed.

EFFECTIVELY MAINTAINING PLANT AND EQUIPMENT

Productivity can be influenced greatly by the effectiveness of the plant and equipment that is available to the first line supervisor. If the plant available is inadequate or inappropriate for the purpose for which it is intended, then output will be reduced, the motivation of the team will be adversely affected and there may be an increase in the potential hazards associated with the work.

First line supervisors therefore have to give careful consideration to the appropriateness of the plant and equipment requisitioned and its regular inspection and maintenance during use. In most organizations there are specialists with responsibility for plant management and servicing, and they provide assistance to supervisors in the selection of appropriate equipment for use on specialized tasks. In addition it may be necessary to hire plant and equipment, and in these cases responsibilities for plant safety and servicing may not be so clear. There are a number of issues that first line supervisors should consider when arranging for the effective maintenance and servicing of plant and equipment. These include:

PLANT MAIN-TENANCE – SOME BASIC ISSUES

- checking to see what the hire agreement contains regarding servicing and inspections
- checking to see whether statutory tests have to be made and appropriate certificates issued before the equipment is ready to use
- checking whether the manufacturer's handbook contains guidance on inspections, tests and regular maintenance
- determining whether the plant will be subjected to continual and heavy use, and if so whether supplementary or more frequent servicing is required
- establishing whether extra tests and inspections are necessary after adverse weather conditions
- keeping proper records of breakdowns, repairs made, servicing provided and the dates when statutory tests and inspections are required and made.

USING NAMED OPERATORS

In many instances there will be routine daily and weekly tasks which have to be completed. It is good practice for the supervisor to ensure that all items of plant have a named operator, who is trained and competent to undertake all these routine checks and maintenance tasks. It will, of course, be necessary for the first line supervisor to see that these checks and tests have been completed and that proper records are kept. Where it is not possible to identify and appoint a member of the team for such tasks, then either the supervisor must undertake the work or regular visits will be required from someone with the necessary special qualification and experience. It is necessary for the supervisor to see that the appropriate records are maintained of all these visits, tests, inspections, servicing and repairs.

SUMMARY

Many construction sites and workshops demonstrate excessive wastage levels of materials, and expensive plant and equipment is regularly abused. These are the all too common signs of inadequate and uncaring supervision. The responsibilities given to first line supervisors regarding materials, plant and equipment may vary from one organization to another, but most first line supervisors will have some responsibilities for calculating or checking quantities of materials, for taking or checking site dimensions, for considering the appropriate allowances for waste, for requisitioning plant and equipment, for inspecting, unloading and proper storage arrangements for materials, plant and equipment and for the effective maintenance of plant. Wherever possible first line supervisors should make use of the specialist skills regarding materials, plant and equipment that are available to them within their employing organizations.

FURTHER STUDY OPPORTUNITIES

The following give a more detailed examination of issues associated with materials, plant and equipment:

CHANDLER, I. E., *Materials Management on Building Sites*, The Construction Press 1978

DOUGHTY, R., *Scaffolding*, Longman Group UK 1986

JOHNSTON, J. E., *Site Control of Materials*, Butterworths 1983

HARRIS, F., *Construction Plant*, Excavating and materials handling equipment and methods, Granada 1981

MEAD, H. T. and MITCHELL, G. L., *Plant Hire for Building and Construction*, Newnes-Butterworth 1972

SKERM, W. C., *A Survey of Materials Handling Procedures*, Heating and Ventilating Research Association 1970

SKOYLES, E. R. and SKOYLES, J. R., *Waste Prevention on Site*, The Mitchell Publishing Company 1987

VALLINGS, H. G., *Mechanisation in Building*, Applied Science Publishers 1975

CHAPTER TEN

PROGRAMMING AND PROGRESSING CONSTRUCTION WORK

This chapter concentrates on short term programming, which should be the principal concern and interest of first line supervisors.

CONSTRUCTION PROGRAMMING

Construction work requires the safe and efficient combination of human resources with materials, plant and equipment, usually in collaboration with other workers, with the objective of meeting the requirements of the contract and achieving acceptable profit margins. This seldom occurs by chance. Therefore, attention must be directed to the sequence in which construction work is undertaken, and the resources which should be allocated to the tasks within each sequence. This process is called construction programming or construction planning. Construction programming is not a once-for-all process as programmes should be produced at different stages in the life of a project. The most frequently used programmes are those designed to:

COMMON FORMS OF PROGRAMMES	<ul><li>co-ordinate the pre-tendering stage</li><li>show the proposed sequence of events upon which the tender was based</li><li>show the principal tasks for the whole project in the form of a master programme</li><li>show as short term programmes, the detailed stages of the work for limited periods of time ranging from a few days to a few weeks.</li></ul>

SHORT TERM PROGRAMMES

Short term, or stage, programmes generally look no more than one month ahead. The purpose of each short term programme is to show what, when, how and in which order the tasks will be sequenced, allocating human resources, plant and materials to these tasks and communicating that information to those involved. Programmes also provide opportunities to check the actual progress of the work and to highlight instances where action is necessary to correct deviations from the intended programme.

The preparation and use of short term programmes requires careful consideration of a number of issues including:

PREPARING SHORT TERM PROG- RAMMES INVOLVES . . .	• checking the contract requirements • determining the preferred sequence of operations • selecting appropriate working methods • allocating appropriate resources • determining appropriate output rates • considering appropriate incentives • allocating adequate supervision • monitoring performance • communicating short term programmes to those involved • action required when work is delayed or changes are required.

Each of these aspects of short term programming is now considered.

Checking the contract requirements

Construction contracts are complex in at least two respects. First, there are usually many contract documents to consider and secondly, it is possible, within the terms of the contract, to make changes as the work proceeds.

Therefore it is necessary to check that each short term programme takes into account all the current contract requirements including:

SHORT TERM PROGRAM- MES SHOULD CONSIDER . . .	• all the **properly authorized drawings** for the work, including the latest revisions of earlier drawings, and drawings produced by specialists which should be approved by the client's agent before issue • any **written variations** to the work, and it is important to recognize that variations can add, delete or change the requirements for any aspect of the work. • any **oral instructions** which have been issued but which have not been confirmed in writing at the time the programme is prepared.

It is also important to identify any uncertainties or unresolved problems which are known about at this time. Therefore each short term programme should be based upon an agreed set of contract requirements.

On some projects, where there are many revisions to the drawings and associated Architect's or Engineer's Instructions issued as the work proceeds, identifying and keeping track of these revisions is a major task in the preparation of effective short term programmes. It is therefore essential to recognize that effective short term programmes must be based upon the complete set of precise contract requirements that relate to the work in hand as these are known at the time each programme is prepared.

Determining the preferred sequence of operations

The expected outcome of the process of checking the contract requirements is to determine the set of tasks which should be included within each short term programme. Some of these tasks will have already started and may be completed during the period of the next short term programme, some will be on-going for several months, some will be new tasks to be completed within this programme, and others will start during the programme but extend beyond it. It is important that each work team has a clearly defined set of tasks with agreed starting and finishing dates shown where these are appropriate and significant.

However, it is necessary to make allowances for bad weather, for sickness and for completing some tasks more quickly, or more slowly, than anticipated. Therefore each short term programme should include rather more tasks than the anticipated minimum number that should be completed within the time available. This means that it is necessary to identify which are the essential tasks which must be completed within the period, and which tasks could be included if there was an opportunity or if something else was delayed.

Thus, these lists of tasks, each with its own order of priority and each related to a specific work group, must be incorporated into a preferred sequence of co-ordinated operations. There are two important issues for the first line supervisor to consider here; first it is necessary to identify potential problems regarding overcrowded work places. For example, it may not be possible for several tasks to be completed at the same time because it is not safe to accommodate all the work groups on the same scaffold or in one area of the site at the same time. Secondly, several tasks may need to use the same items of plant, such as tower cranes, hoists, circular saw or spindle moulder at the same time and this would produce bottle necks in the work. Therefore it is necessary to consider both the **sequence of tasks** within each work group, and the **interactions of these sequences** between the different work groups.

Selecting appropriate working methods

In some instances basic working methods may have been decided at an earlier stage in the project. For instance, decisions about which items of large mechanical plant to use are normally determined at the tender stage, and therefore such decisions limit the range of options available. However, it is important to use the opportunities provided at each short term planning stage to consider all the available options and then to select the most appropriate. This may require collaboration between programmers, first line supervisors, plant managers and surveyors so that there is agreement on the cost effectiveness of the selected methods.

Allocating appropriate resources

Once agreement has been reached on the appropriate working methods it is necessary to allocate resources to them. The obvious resources are human resources or 'labour', materials and plant.

With human resources there are two principal issues to consider, these are **the gang size** and the **working hours available** during the period of the programme. Once the working methods have been agreed, the minimum gang sizes can be determined. It is often undesirable to have widely fluctuating gang sizes, because this means people have to be transferred frequently to and from each task. Therefore it is usually sufficient to ensure that the gang sizes are above the minimum required to complete the essential tasks within normal working hours. This is because it is necessary to consider whether all the members of each team will be available throughout the period of the programme. There are holidays and training courses to consider, and some allowance should be made for absence due to sickness. Allowances for lost time may also have to be made because of the weather, or because of the need to restrict working hours for some reason, such as working in occupied buildings. Special attention should be given to the need for special skills during the period and whether there are sufficient people available with the required skills to complete the work within the period.

Materials need to be carefully considered during the preparation of short term programmes. Each first line supervisor needs to check that all materials and components are already available or will be delivered to meet the requirements of the programme. In some instances, great care is needed to ensure that work is not delayed because of the lack of small but essential items. Therefore it will often be necessary to provide precise schedules of the components and materials required for the work and to check that these are already available, that deliveries have been arranged to meet the programme requirements or that the items can be bought locally and are within the first line supervisor's authority and budget for local purchases.

Similar checks are necessary regarding **plant**, particularly powered or specialized hand tools. Major plant items are relatively easy to check out, it is the small items that require careful attention. Much time and effort can be wasted either in trying to find a local tool hire firm with the appropriate equipment immediately available, or in making do with inappropriate equipment.

Determining appropriate output rates

Some organizations will have schedules of output rates prepared for programming or for bonus payment purposes. These may not cover every item of work within each short term programme but they may cover the major tasks. The following are some examples of the output rates used by one organization:

SOME EXAMPLES OF OUTPUT RATES	• build half brick skin of cavity wall in selected facing bricks, including wall ties, on prepared surface in cement mortar 1.80 hours/square metre • take out old wash hand basin and renew with new taps, brackets, waste and connect to existing water supply and waste pipe 3.50 hours/wash basin • prepare and apply two coats of oil or polyurethane paint or varnish to door or window as specified 1.50 hours/face

Such output rates, and they may differ widely between organizations, may provide a means of calculating the amount of work which can reasonably be completed within the period of the short term programme. For instance, assuming that 550 square metres of half brick skin to a cavity wall was programmed to be completed within four weeks, this operation would take 990 hours of a bricklayer's time using the above output figures. Allowing a 40 hour working week this task would occupy six bricklayers for the full four weeks.

Different organizations will use different output rates, and many first line supervisors have developed their own output criteria on which they can assess the amount of work their team will complete within a given period. It is virtually impossible to prepare accurate short term programmes without having some data on output rates. Schedules of such rates for the most common tasks can be built up and agreed relatively quickly without using complex work study techniques. It is a reasonably simple matter for a first line supervisor to mark up a drawing with the main areas of work completed each week, to scale these off the drawings in order to calculate the areas or volumes of work completed, and to divide these by the number of hours the team members spend as recorded on their time sheets. If this exercise is completed for several weeks and the results averaged out, a reasonably accurate output figure for each of the main tasks can be obtained within two months.

Most difficulties arise with one-off tasks for which no-one has any previous experience. In such situations often all that can be done is to make a best guess at the likely rate of output, and to monitor performance carefully as the work proceeds.

Considering appropriate incentives

Performance related financial incentives have had a somewhat chequered history in the British construction industry during the last 30 years. Sometimes they have been almost non existent and at other times legislation has encouraged their use in order to link increases in pay with increases in output. Work study based incentive schemes assume that operatives whose performance is 'standard' should have their earnings increased by a third. There are many reasons why work study based incentive schemes currently do not feature highly in the British construction industry. These include the:

- variety of work and working conditions in the industry
- large number of small projects
- increase in self employment and sub-contracting
- high costs of administering incentive schemes.

Many employers now use **plus rates**, **standing bonus schemes**, or **group schemes** in which profit or the benefits from increased levels of output are shared more or less equally between all members of a work team. These simplified schemes reduce the administrative costs of work study based schemes. In projects where time is of the essence, financial incentives have often been used in order to encourage a higher than average output.

First line supervisors need to consider some of the adverse consequences of using financial incentives, including:

SOME ADVERSE FEATURES OF FINANCIAL INCENTIVES	• possible reductions in quality standards • a tendency for tasks which require high levels of personal skill to result in lower than average bonus earnings • lack of interest in low bonus earning tasks • higher levels of wastage in the use of materials • less attention paid to health and safety precautions • less attention paid to tidiness • low standards of workmanship on tasks which are subsequently covered up.

These issues often mean that more supervision is required when incentive schemes are in use than would otherwise be the case. Therefore, when preparing short term programmes, careful consideration should be given to the relative advantages and disadvantages of performance based incentive schemes. It may be more effective to use a higher basic rate, or to offer some overtime in order to complete specific tasks in the limited times available.

Allocating adequate supervision

When the tasks to be incorporated in a short term programme have been identified, the appropriate resources allocated and the preferred output rates established, it will be necessary to allocate adequate supervision to ensure that the work is completed within acceptable quality standards. There are a number of areas where first line supervisors can become overstretched when high levels of output are required. These include:

INCENTIVE SCHEMES – THE SUPERVISORY REQUIREMENTS	<ul><li>making time available in order to explain the work properly to each member of the team</li><li>checking that materials are available when required</li><li>arranging for all plant and equipment to be available</li><li>making routine inspections so that potential health and safety hazards can be identified</li><li>maintaining appropriate quality standards</li><li>seeing that the levels of materials waste are kept within agreed limits.</li></ul>

It may be necessary for first line supervisors to arrange for some temporary assistance during those periods when high levels of output are required, or when work teams are needed to meet demanding deadlines. Additional help may also be needed from storekeepers and safety officers, or it may be necessary to arrange for a member of the work team to be appointed as a temporary chargehand for a period. In all such cases it is necessary to determine the precise tasks required of such helpers, and to ensure that all members of the team understand what is happening and why temporary changes have been made to the working arrangements.

Monitoring performance

There is no point whatsoever in producing short term programmes unless they are used as the basis of a system of performance monitoring and unless the progress achieved is reported back regularly to those concerned. Using an earlier example, if a team of six bricklayers is required to complete 550 square metres of brickwork in four weeks, then the daily output of the team would be some 27 square metres of brickwork. If the actual output each day was much lower than this then the reasons should be investigated. If the reasons are justified, because of poor weather conditions or perhaps because two members of the team were absent that week, then it may be necessary to consider how to bring the performance back in line with the programme. This may be achieved by working overtime, or by bringing in extra bricklayers for a short period.

On the other hand, if output considerably exceeds the daily target of 27 square metres, the supervisor will need to bring additional tasks forward into the programme otherwise the team will run out of work. So the programme provides a statement of the preferred plan to be used in order to meet the contract requirements. Sometimes the actual outputs achieved will require modifications to the programme. Where output is higher than anticipated, other work can be brought forward. Where output is less than anticipated, the work team may need to be increased in size, overtime worked or special incentives offered.

However, it is not always desirable to keep bringing work forward when output is higher than anticipated. Work can get out of sequence, delivery schedules can be disrupted and the work of other teams can be adversely affected. Therefore deviations from the programme should be carefully monitored, and the longer term implications considered before allowing such deviations to continue unchecked.

Communicating short term programmes to those involved

It is essential to get the commitment of first line supervisors to short term programmes because they have the responsibility for seeing that the programmes are implemented. Therefore it is usual to involve the appropriate first line supervisors in the preparation of each short term programme. Other members of the line management team will also be involved as will the surveyor and anyone with special programming skills. There will be occasions when specialist skills are required to consider the implications associated with critical or unusual tasks.

Therefore each short term programme is usually the subject of a meeting, to which all the key people are invited and expected to participate in the preparation of the programme. The outcome of such meetings will be a draft programme which should be distributed for comments before any final adjustments are made and the programme formally issued.

Short term programmes can be presented in several forms. Perhaps the most common form is a **simple bar chart** in which each task is shown as a separate bar. This technique is very satisfactory where the tasks are easily recognized with simple short descriptions. Where the tasks within the programme are more complex, or inter-related with other work, it may be necessary to present them as a **schedule of operations** in which each task is described in some detail, together with the plant and materials allocated for the work. Each item on the schedule can be given a reference number and these numbers used for allocating the time spent by members of the team to each task. Sometimes, when the task is very repetitive, it is more appropriate to present the programme in the form of a **diagram or sketch** of the work showing the sequence in which bays or elements of the work are to be completed, and indicating on the diagram the starting and finishing dates for each element.

Clearly the first time supervisor, and other members of the management team with responsibilities for the work, should have copies of each programme, and should be involved in discussions regarding the appropriate actions to take when performance deviates from the programme. However, it is not always so easy to decide whether the members of the work team should be similarly involved in the preparation and monitoring of the programme.

Where the management style is **participative**, and all employees are encouraged to share in the preparation of work programmes, then it follows that each work team would be actively involved in programming and in monitoring performance.

Where the management style is **autocratic or power based**, then employees would only be informed of what they need to know in order to do their jobs satisfactorily from a management point of view. In such organizations it is unusual for the team members to receive copies of short team programmes. The first line supervisors would be expected to allocate tasks on a daily basis to each member of the team, and there would be limited feedback to the team members on the progress of the work.

Action when work is delayed or changes are required

One of the purposes of short term programmes is to show how management intended the work to be organized in order to meet the requirements of the contract as these were understood at the time each programme was prepared. Programmes are expected to include allowances for anticipated delays and other perceived uncertainties. However, short term programmes cannot make allowances for totally unexpected events. Therefore occasionally a programme will be prepared in good faith but events will occur which will make it impossible to meet the requirements of the programmes. These events might include:

SOME
REASONS
WHY WORK
MAY BE
DELAYED

- severe storms
- the bankruptcy of key sub-contractors or suppliers
- major changes required by the client
- strikes or other unexpected withdrawal of key personal services
- transport difficulties or power disruptions outside the control of the parties concerned.

When problems such as these do arise it will be necessary to record the current state of the progress of the work. Therefore regular performance monitoring and recording of progress is essential. It may also be necessary to produce a new programme showing how the adverse effects of these problems can be overcome with the least delay and increases in cost. Sometimes it is not possible to make an immediate assessment of the full implications of the problems, and work has to be suspended until the picture becomes clear. Unless there has been an established discipline of short term programming, and regular recording of the progress of the work, it will be very difficult to make an accurate assessment of the remedial actions necessary when major problems occur.

SUMMARY

Thus it is essential to recognize that short term programmes are more important when uncertainty is highest and the project is beset with problems. Unfortunately under these conditions programming is often abandoned and supervisors try and muddle through by doing those tasks which seem clearly defined and for which resources are available, only to find at some later date that changes have to be made and all the costs of making these changes may not be easily recoverable. So short term programming requires careful consideration by first line supervisors to the contract requirements, to the availability of resources and to the output of the team. The progress of the work requires careful monitoring and line management should be informed of the problems which are encountered in trying to meet the requirements of short term programmes. Remember that getting too far ahead of the programme can be just as problematic as falling a long way behind.

FURTHER STUDY OPPORTUNITIES

The following give a more detailed treatment of construction programming techniques

ARMSTRONG, B., *Programming Building Contracts*, Northwood Books 1981

BURGESS, R. A. and WHITE, G., *Building Production and Project Management*, The Construction Press 1979

CALVERT, R. E., *Introduction to Building Management*, Butterworths 1981

CIOB, *Programmes in Construction*, A guide to good practice, Chartered Institute of Building 1980

DREWIN, F. J., *Construction Productivity*, Measurement and improvement through work study, Elsevier 1982

HOLLINS, R. J., *Production and Planning Applied to Building*, George Godwin 1971

ILO, *Introduction to Work Study*, Geneva, Switzerland, International Labour Office 1974

OXLEY, R. and POSKITT, J., *Management Techniques Applied to the Construction Industry*, Granada, 3rd edition 1980

CHAPTER ELEVEN

THE ORGANIZATION OF THE WORKPLACE

This chapter considers some of the issues associated with laying out the workplace, problems regarding inclement weather, leaving the workplace safe and secure at the end of each work period, and some of the security issues associated with working in occupied buildings.

TYPES OF WORKPLACE

Often the workplace is a major factor when first line supervisors consider the issues associated with organizing work. The workplace may be a bespoke and long established workshop, a construction site or an occupied building.

When considering the organization of work in a **workshop**, the supervisor has to balance the often conflicting interests of the individual members of the work team, the requirements of specific contracts and the most efficient sequence of operations for each project, with the restrictions imposed by space and machinery. On a **new construction site** some tasks may take just a few moments to complete and others may require many weeks of work in a particular location. Thus on most new construction sites the work place is a shifting scene with all the obvious implications this has for access, communications and safety. Finally, the work place may be in an **occupied building** and therefore the workplace has to be shared by the occupants and the work team. This raises additional problems associated with access, nuisance, safety and security.

WORKSHOP LAYOUT

Few workshop based supervisors ever have the opportunity to lay out a complete workshop from first principles. Therefore in most cases decisions will have already been made and actions taken which have restricted the range of options available to a first line supervisor. Many of the existing larger machines will have fixed locations and new or replacement equipment will normally have to be fitted in where space is available.

Many workshops associated with the construction industry specialize in small batches of work for specific contracts, rather than in long production runs of specialized products. It is also normal for several projects each with unique characteristics to be in the workshop at the same time, with each project at a different stage of production. This means that it is difficult to arrange a workshop layout that will be ideally suited to the specific requirements of all these different projects. The following issues may need to be considered:

WORKSHOP LAYOUT – SOME BASIC ISSUES	• the identification of the tasks involved in each project • the sequence in which those tasks need to be completed • the machines required for each stage of the work • the time required to complete each task • the number of different projects in the workshop at the same time • the bottle-necks likely to result from the different needs of each project • the extent to which particular tasks can be speeded up, delayed, allocated to different machines, or sub-contracted out in order to minimize bottle-neck problems • the extent to which design changes can be introduced in order to smooth out production problems • whether additional projects can be introduced in order to ensure that specific machines are kept in full production, or to reduce the need for retooling.

All these issues can be made more complex by holidays, sickness, machine breakdowns, design changes and the non delivery of materials, and some of these issues will be outside the control of the supervisor.

WORKSHOP ORGANIZATION – ESSENTIAL FACTORS

There are several essential factors about workshop organization that first line supervisors need to consider. These include obtaining advanced notice of new projects, and having the time, or specialized resources to:

WORKSHOP ORGANIZA-TION – SOME BASIC ISSUES	• plan and quantify all the stages of the work associated with each project • check the availability of all the materials and specialized tools required • plan the sequence of operations involved in processing the project through the workshop, and in so doing to identify any potential hazards associated with the work and plan the appropriate precautions necessary to guard against those hazards • establish the preferred completion date and to make any modifications necessary to the work programme in order to meet contract requirements

- communicate the details of the work to those concerned and to provide any necessary training and support needed
- monitor the progress of the work and take action to resolve unforeseen problems as these arise.

In order to undertake these tasks effectively, it is necessary to have a lead-in period for each job, and in the larger workshops to have some assistance with programming and scheduling, so that work can be batched together with minimum conflicts and bottle-necks.

CONSTRUCTION SITE LAYOUT

Organizing the workplace on new construction sites presents different problems. These are mainly the result of the speed of the construction process and the transitory nature of the workplace. The sequence of site operations will usually change the nature of the workplace for each successive work team. This means that each first line supervisor will be attempting to organize the workplace before it exists, and will be relying on other teams to provide a safe place in which to work. Thus each first line supervisor will need to communicate the following issues to site management:

SITE LAYOUT
– SOME BASIC
ISSUES

- the time when the workplace should be ready for work to start
- the minimum storage areas necessary for plant materials
- access arrangements to the workplace, including any temporary access such as scaffolding
- materials handling arrangements, where these are to be provided by others, or where specialist plant is necessary
- the specialist electrical power or temporary lighting needs together with any specialist services required
- the potential safety and health hazards associated with the work, and the restrictions that should be placed on the access to the workplace by others when work is in progress
- any time lapses which might be needed for drying or curing times, following the completion of the work and before other work teams can have access to the same workplace
- any arrangements that are required for clearing rubbish or surplus materials from the workplace.

SITE ORGANIZATION – ESSENTIAL FACTORS

In principle, there are three major requirements associated with the organization of workplaces on new construction sites that need to be considered by first line supervisors. These are:

SITE ORGA-NIZATION – SOME BASIC ISSUES

- the need to make known their minimum requirements sufficiently far in advance of work starting so that others can make the necessary arrangements
- to ensure that any hazards associated with their work are communicated effectively to site management and appropriate precautions taken to safeguard other site workers, this might involve restricting access to the workplace by, for instance, providing permits to work in hazardous areas
- to ensure that site management is informed of all instances where work is delayed, is likely to be completed more quickly than anticipated, or where unforeseen problems have arisen which might have implications for the work of other teams.

WORKPLACE LAYOUT IN OCCUPIED BUILDINGS

Where the workplace is in an occupied building, the first line supervisor will normally have to consider a wider range of issues. These include:

WORK IN OCCUPIED BUILDINGS – SOME BASIC ISSUES

- seeing that occupants are properly informed of the nature of the work and of any restrictions which will affect their use of the building
- seeing that proper arrangements have been made and agreed with occupants regarding access for members of the work team, storage of materials and plant
- agreeing working hours, noise levels and other necessary disturbances
- making special arrangements where there are particularly vulnerable occupants, such as elderly or disabled people, children or animals.

It is essential that first line supervisors recognize that most of the occupants of buildings in which work has to take place, will see any construction work as an inconvenience and a disruption of their normal lives. Careful preparation is therefore essential to ensure that workplaces are planned well in advance and the occupants properly prepared for the work.

ADVERSE WEATHER AND THE WORKPLACE

Special precautions are necessary where the workplace is exposed to the weather. These precautions take three principal forms:

ADVERSE WEATHER – SOME BASIC ISSUES	• the need for appropriate protective clothing to be readily available for every member of the work team • to consider what precautions should be taken to protect the work from damage • to consider the effect adverse weather might have upon the safety of the workplace. Particularly the effects of wind, snow and ice on scaffolding, and the flooding of excavations, basements and sewers.

Attention should be paid to:

WEATHER – SOME SUPERVISORY ACTIONS	• using weather forecasts to predict weather conditions • providing alternative work in protected workplaces wherever possible when bad weather is forecast • ensuring that work does not continue when there are obvious hazards, for instance sewer maintenance should not continue when thunderstorms or heavy rain are imminent • ensuring that the workplace is properly inspected before work resumes after a break for bad weather. This is essential where scaffolding or shoring may have been disturbed by rain, ice or gale force winds.

PRE-INSPECTIONS OF THE WORKPLACE

First line supervisors should inspect the workplace before work starts each morning. This is especially important during winter months on exposed building sites. Snow and ice on scaffold boards and roof surfaces are obvious hazards and the thoughtful supervisor can often organize the workplace so that the most exposed tasks are not undertaken in the worst weather.

Where the workplace is a factory or an occupied building, there are few additional precautions to take other than those which are obvious, such as minimum working temperatures. The supervisor may need to ensure that central heating controls are set so that the minimum temperature is reached at the start of the working day.

WORKPLACE SECURITY

It is essential, particularly when working in occupied buildings, to ensure that the workplace is left secure at the end of each work period. There are three sets of security issues to consider:

- the physical security of the workplace against **illegal entry**
- precautions against **fire** and accidental **flooding**
- the removal of obvious **health** and **safety** hazards.

Physical security of the workplace

First line supervisors must be aware of the need to ensure that the workplace is physically secure at the end of each work period, particularly when operatives leave the area. It is important that the supervisor should inspect the workplace at the end of the period of work to:

SECURITY INSPECTIONS	<ul><li>see that all doors and windows are shut and locked</li><li>check that where burglar alarms exist they have been properly set</li><li>ensure that ladders are removed from the lower scaffold stages</li><li>immobilize or remove from view all plant and equipment that could be used to gain entrance to buildings</li><li>ensure that hand tools have been removed to a place of safety and locked up.</li></ul>

Where there are security guards or resident caretakers they should be kept informed of the areas where there are high security risks and the precise arrangements to be made at the end of each work shift should be agreed with them. On large projects, where the arrangements may be complex, end of shift procedures should be formalized into check lists and the inspections made jointly with security staff. The results of each inspection should be entered into a record book.

Construction work often presents major security risks because of the changing nature of the work and the ready availability of ladders, scaffolding and cutting equipment at or near the workplace.

Damage from accidental fire and flooding

Precautions also need to be taken to reduce the risk of damage from fire and flooding which may happen as a consequence of construction work. In high fire risk areas smoking and naked lights should be banned. This may mean that working methods have to be revised, for example to avoid the use of blow lamps inside roof spaces. Where workplaces are located inside old buildings smoke detectors should be placed in all high risk areas. There should be regular assessments made of fire risks and the precautions to be taken during work shifts and outside working hours.

Attention also needs to be paid to the avoidance of accidental flooding. This can be problematic when:

AVOID POSSIBLE FLOODING WHEN . . .	• roof repairs are in progress • rain water pipes and surface water drains are being installed or repaired • buildings are left unheated during winter months • taps and hose pipes are left running without proper supervision • water supply and drainage services have been temporarily disconnected • pipe work may have been accidentally damaged during other work • materials are stacked so that they block rain water gullies • rubbish is allowed to accumulate blocking drains and gutters.

It is particularly important for supervisors to recognize the additional accidental flood hazards that can result from working on or adjacent to the plumbing and drainage services in unoccupied buildings, and from heavy storms which may occur outside working hours. Care must always be taken to ensure that materials are not spoilt because of inadequate protection against damage by water. Temporary roof coverings should be checked at the end of each work shift. It may be necessary to make special visits to the site outside normal working hours, at weekends and when the site is closed down for public holidays, to ensure that temporary roof coverings remain in place and that no damage is occurring to the fabric because of heavy rain or water penetration.

Health and safety hazards

It is also necessary for first line supervisors to check that no obvious health or safety hazards remain at the end of each work shift. This is of particular importance when working inside occupied buildings. There are a number of obvious checks to be made by supervisors. These include:

HEALTH AND SAFETY HAZARDS – SUPERVISORY CHECKS	• removing powered hand tools and other small items of mechanical plant to locked stores • immobilizing all large items of plant • disconnecting power leads and temporary wiring • ensuring that all electrical services are left safe to use • checking that there are no unprotected holes in floors, walls or balustrades • checking that all hazardous materials have been removed to the stores

> • ensuring that access is restricted to areas of the site where there are special hazards, including excavations, scaffolding and roofs and that warning notices are displayed as appropriate.

A DUTY TO WARN OTHERS OF MAJOR HAZARDS

Where there are very high health or safety risks associated with the work and where it is very difficult to prevent unauthorized access to the workplace outside normal working hours, it may be necessary to make special arrangements. Many of these arrangements are expensive to introduce and would be beyond the normal responsibilities of first line supervisors. However, all first line supervisors have a responsibility to warn their senior managers of any major hazards associated with their work and to seek the specialist help of safety officers. In addition it may be possible for first line supervisors to inform:

SUPERVISORS MAY CONSIDER WARNINGS TO . . .	• occupants of the hazards associated with the work so that children are kept away from the workplace • caretakers of any special hazards and the precautions that have been taken to protect the public against injury • police or neighbourhood watch organizers of any special hazards.

REGULAR INSPECTIONS

It is impossible to guard against every remote and unlikely hazard, but all supervisors should recognize that they are expected to take precautions against obvious hazards where the risks of injury are high. Regular inspections of the workplace are essential. Supervisors must be aware of the hazards associated with the use of the materials and plant for the contract works. Supervisors must read the guidance notes and handbooks provided by manufacturers and if they are in any doubt about the proper precautions to be taken, they must seek specialist advice before work starts.

ORGANIZATIONAL SECURITY

There will be occasions when the workplace is located inside buildings and where restrictions may be placed upon those seeking access for construction work. These restrictions may be necessary because of:

RESTRIC-TIONS TO ACCESS BE-CAUSE OF . . .	• the **contents of the building**, or the activities which take place inside the area; for instance, restrictions may be placed upon those working inside banks or military establishments

- the existence of **special health or safety hazards** in the area, for example restrictions may be placed upon those working in close proximity to railway lines, power cables or inside research establishments
- the **vulnerability of the occupants**, where there may need to be restrictions placed upon those working in buildings occupied by the very old or the very young.

Contract requirements

In such cases it is normal for the contract documents to lay down the procedures to be followed. These procedures may require:

SECURITY – SOME CONTRACTURAL REQUIRE- MENTS	• the names, addresses and some other personal details of all those who will be working on the project to be submitted to the client, or the client's security advisers, some weeks in advance of the work starting

- personal identity cards with photographs to be prepared and authorized for each person approved to work on the project
- advanced notice of entry to specified areas, and for workers to be accompanied when in high security areas
- showing personal identity cards on each occasion entry to a designated area is required, and on all other occasions on request
- preliminary specialized safety training to be undertaken before permits to work in hazardous areas are issued
- special protective clothing to be worn when working in specified areas
- special decontamination procedures to be followed when leaving designated areas
- regular health checks during and following prolonged working in such areas
- signing an agreement to comply with specified procedures and an acceptance of specified penalties for non compliance.

ISSUES FOR THE FIRST LINE SUPERVISOR

First line supervisors have a responsibility to see that all the members of their work teams understand and abide by the necessary procedures. This is not always as easy as it sounds. There are special problems when:

SECURITY – THE SUPERVISORY PROBLEMS	• there is a high mobility of labour or where many changes in the work force are necessary • changes in contract requirements require immediate changes in the sequence of operations and the composition of work teams • sub-contractors change their work teams without notice • individual employees refuse to provide the necessary personal details or where the client refuses to give security clearance to key operatives.

In many such projects the first line supervisor's employer will need to make special insurance arrangements to cover for the increased risks associated with such work. These arrangements will often carry special procedures in the event of any claims under the terms of the insurance. It is important that first line supervisors know of these procedures, and do not reduce the potential benefits to be gained from the insurance policy through ignorance or deliberate non-compliance with the agreed procedures.

SUMMARY

Construction workplaces may be workshops, construction sites or occupied buildings. First line supervisors may therefore have several different settings within which to consider the layout and organization of the workplaces to be used by their teams, and special considerations may arise where these workplaces are exposed to adverse weather.

First line supervisors will need, from time to time, to consider the security of workplaces, particularly regarding illegal entry, accidental fire and flooding and the health and safety hazards which may arise as a consequence of construction work. Also, the first line supervisor may need to consider the restrictions placed upon the access of construction workers to their workplaces because of the nature of the contents of the buildings, the special health and safety hazards associated with the processes being undertaken within those buildings or because of the vulnerability of the occupants

FURTHER STUDY OPPORTUNITIES

CHARLETT, A. J., *Security of Building Sites*, Occasional Paper no 33, Chartered Institute of Building nd

CHARLETT, A. J., *Vandalism and Trespass by Children on Building Sites*, Technical Information Paper no 60, Chartered Institute of Building nd

EARNSHAW, L., *Construction Site Security*, Construction Press 1984

EDMEADES, D. H., *The Construction Site*, The Estates Gazette 1972

SANSOM, R. C., *Organization of Building Sites*, HMSO 1959

CHAPTER TWELVE

SETTING-OUT RESPONSIBILITIES

This chapter examines some of the basic issues associated with first line supervisory responsibilities for setting-out, including equipment, working from accurate instructions and from appropriate control points and grid lines, checking any setting-out done by others, taking site dimensions, deciding on appropriate manufacturing tolerances and keeping adequate records of setting-out activities.

SUPERVISORY RESPONSIBILITIES FOR SETTING-OUT

First line supervisors will usually have some responsibilities for setting-out. These responsibilities may include using jigs, patterns and templates in workshops, taking site dimensions in order to pre-fabricate components off site for site fixing at some later stage, setting-out on site for elements of new construction or alteration work, and setting-out for temporary works or preparatory investigations. Seldom will first line supervisors be responsible for surveying the whole sites or for setting-out complete buildings. Therefore most of the setting-out done by first line supervisors will be secondary in nature, and will be set within some existing framework of lines or structure.

SETTING-OUT EQUIPMENT

The equipment required for setting-out will vary according to the nature of the work and the size of the project. There is no standard setting-out kit for construction work. Therefore each first line supervisor will need to think in advance about the nature of the work and the setting-out equipment required and to arrange for it to be available. This is particularly important where it is necessary to visit a site, which may be some distance from the workshop, to take site dimensions.

There are, however, some basic items of equipment that all first line supervisors should always have available, and these include:

SETTING-OUT – THE BASIC EQUIPMENT	• notebook and pencil • steel tapes – 3 and 30 metres in length • plumb lines • straight edge

> • setting-out or builder's square
> • spirit and water levels.

There will also be a need for some other items, including of course, safety equipment and perhaps torches and a camera. With very complex setting-out more specialized equipment may be required, including:

- gauge rods and profile gauges
- bevels
- optical square
- trammels.

SPECIAL SETTING-OUT EQUIPMENT

It is rare for first line supervisors to need dumpy levels, although occasionally they may be required to assist others with setting-out work which involves the use of theodolite, electromagnetic distance measuring equipment, optical levels and lasers. It is important to recognize that setting-out equipment must be accurate and must be checked for accuracy before use. There are simple tests for checking the accuracy of tapes, squares and spirit levels. With some other equipment the tests are more complex and many organizations arrange for their setting-out equipment to be regularly tested by specialists. It is a basic rule of setting-out that any measuring equipment required should be checked for accuracy before use.

WORKING FROM ACCURATE INSTRUCTIONS

One of the most time consuming activities associated with setting-out is ensuring that all the instructions are available, that there are no discrepancies between the various documents and that there is enough information to set the work out without ambiguity. There are four basic rules to follow:

SETTING-OUT – THE BASIC RULES	• identify **all the documents** that contain information about the work and remove those that have been superseded, get any discrepancies contractually resolved before setting-out starts • work only from stated **dimensions** • if it is necessary to **prepare setting-out drawings** or diagrams these must be dated and state the references and dates of issue of all the drawings, specifications, written instructions used to prepare the diagrams • get someone else to make an **independent check** of the diagram before setting-out starts.

Construction work is bedevilled by instances where work has been set-out from obsolete drawings, or where supervisors have resolved discrepancies for themselves. It is therefore vitally important to ensure that all setting-out is based on the contract data available at the time, and if this is insufficient to enable the work to be set out with the required accuracy then the additional information should be requested before setting-out takes place.

CONTROL POINTS AND TEMPORARY BENCH MARKS

First line supervisors should always start their setting-out from the nearest control points or lines or from agreed temporary bench marks rather than setting-out from any adjacent work which may be inaccurate. Therefore it will be necessary to find out from site management where the primary setting-out controls are located. For instance, new construction projects may have datums set one metre above the finished floor levels and the primary grid lines may be marked on profile boards or column faces. It may have been necessary to incorporate offset pegs in the original setting-out and these can sometimes be confused with primary control points or spot levels, so first line supervisors should ensure that they have the primary setting-out explained to them and thus minimize any confusion regarding the lines and levels from which to start their own setting-out operations.

CHECKING ANY SETTING-OUT DONE BY OTHERS

In some instances, setting-out may be undertaken by specialists who may or may not be employed within the same organization as the first line supervisor. First line supervisors should check all setting-out before work starts, because it is always easier to correct mistakes in the setting-out than it is to change the dimensions of any component once made, built or fixed. Thus the first line supervisor should:

CHECKING SETTING-OUT – SOME BASIC ISSUES	• have a clear picture of the requirements of the work and particularly of the principal dimensions • make simple visual checks to see that components will line and level-in properly with other work • check the principal dimensions carefully • check any falls, angles or offsets before work starts • use templates or gauge rods to determine the position of key components before work starts • seek advice if any discrepancies become apparent.

It is generally recognized that all important setting-out work should be independently checked before work starts. Most first line supervisors have highly developed skills regarding their own specialist areas of work, and this enables them to recognize speedily some setting-out errors. Therefore first line supervisors can be used as part of the system of checks and controls used to minimize errors.

In such situations, however, it is advisable to ensure that first line supervisors know of the part they are required to play in this respect.

TAKING SITE DIMENSIONS

There are many occasions when site dimensions are required so that components can be manufactured to the required dimensions away from the site. Many components cannot be manufactured with sufficient accuracy from drawings, even when allowances have been made for fitting on site. Examples of such components include staircases, handrails and balustrades, replacement windows and some internal fittings and fixtures.

In order to take the necessary site dimensions, preparatory site work will need to have reached an appropriate stage. Thus the primary requirement is to ensure that the site management team knows that it is necessary to indicate that a stage has been reached in the construction process when site dimensions can be taken. This is often more complex than it sounds. Once site dimensions have been taken, several weeks may be required for manufacture before fixing can start on site. It is therefore necessary to inform site management of the manufacturing time which has to elapse, and any other activities which have to take place, between taking dimensions and site installation.

On projects where speed is of the essence, there will often be major difficulties surrounding site dimensions and off-site manufacturing times, and it is important to ensure that all the essential steps in the process are understood. These should be included in the contract documentation and should be clarified with the site management team well before work is due to start. The essential steps will vary depending upon the nature of the work but may involve:

TAKING SITE DIMENSIONS – SOME BASIC ISSUES	• a statement indicating the preliminary work which has to be completed before site dimensions can be taken • the minimum notice required in which to arrange a site visit to take site dimensions • the equipment, if any, which has to be provided at the time of the visit • checking and approving drawings made subsequent to the site visit • agreeing to undertake further preparatory work or any remedial works prior to manufacture or delivery • agreeing the earliest delivery dates and the facilities required during site fixing.

Usually most of these issues will have been incorporated in the contract documents, but many first line supervisors find that when they arrive on site to take site dimensions, major changes have taken place on site which change their own contractual arrangements, so that contract renegotiations are necessary.

SITE DIMENSIONS – ESSENTIAL STEPS

Taking site dimensions therefore involves the following essential steps:

SITE DIMEN-SIONS – THE ESSENTIAL STEPS	• knowing the precise contract requirements • having travel directions and the name of the site contact • making and confirming an appointment in advance • knowing the precise dimensions to be taken and recorded on site and having these agreed and incorporated into prepared schedules, drawings, sketches or check lists so that no essential information is forgotten • determining whether site dimensions can be taken safely by one person or whether assistance is necessary • taking all appropriate protective clothing and safety equipment • taking all the measuring and setting-out equipment necessary to obtain the required dimensions • taking a camera and tape recorder if possible to record unusual features • taking all appropriate authorization and identity cards in order to gain access, and leaving details with the office of the time anticipated on site • checking on arrival that the site is safe for the purpose of taking dimensions • recording all the relevant contract documents available on to the site • taking and checking all dimensions • leave the site in a safe condition once all dimensions have been taken and checked • check that no equipment has been left behind • ensuring that site management is properly informed at the end of the visit of any problems and discrepancies, and is informed of the need to approve drawings or schedules to be prepared from the visit.

There will be many occasions when things do not turn out as expected, sometimes it is all much easier than anticipated, but more often there are difficulties and uncertainties to overcome. Usually these cannot be resolved during the site visit. It is essential that the site management team is informed that there are issues to be resolved, so that they are not surprised by subsequent events. It is also essential that as many facts as possible are taken from the site, which is where a camera can be useful.

DECIDING ON APPROPRIATE TOLERANCES

Absolute dimensional accuracy in building work is unlikely to be achieved. Some dimensional deviations will therefore occur either because of the inaccuracies of the construction process or because of the characteristics of the materials.

The construction process will contain dimensional inaccuracies for one or more of three principal reasons. First, the manufacturers of measuring equipment indicate the precision that can be achieved if their equipment is in proper adjustment and is used by competent people. None of this equipment is ever absolutely accurate. Secondly, some dimensional inaccuracies will occur during the manufacture of components and materials, these may be inaccuracies in length, thickness, angular measurement or surface irregularity. Thirdly, components of construction may not be located exactly in their designed positions.

PERMITTED DEVIATIONS

It is usual therefore to allow for some permitted deviations between the **design dimensions** and the **actual dimensions** of a piece of work. The size of these permitted deviations will vary from one type of work to another. It is helpful if the permitted dimensional deviations are stated, for instance a dimension might be given as 990 mm + (plus) or − (minus) 10 mm, indicating that the minimum acceptable dimension would be 980 mm and the maximum acceptable dimension 1000 mm and any component in between these dimensions would therefore be acceptable.

JOINT SIZES

There are some dimensional deviations which relate to the nature of the materials and which may be influenced by temperature, moisture content or age. These characteristics should be considered at the design stage. Joint sizes should therefore allow for dimensional changes within the anticipated ranges appropriate for the materials and the environment in which the building will be located. First line supervisors should be aware that many building components are subjected to a greater degree of exposure during the construction process than during most of their useful lives within the completed building. Therefore attention should be directed to limiting dimension deviations, particularly regarding moisture movement, during the construction process.

VISUAL APPEARANCE

Dimensional tolerances have to receive special attention where the appearance of the finished work is important. An obvious example of this relates to faced brickwork, where the thickness of the brickwork joints should not vary excessively. Therefore gauge rods and templates are used to assist bricklayers to maintain joints of an even thickness, and to construct openings of minimum sizes. This allows prefabricated frames to be fixed after the brickwork is complete, without the need for adjustments to the dimensions of either the frame or the opening in the brickwork.

SETTING-OUT TOLERANCES

First line supervisors therefore have to give careful consideration to tolerances when setting-out. Frequently insufficient details are given on drawings regarding appropriate dimensional deviations, and these are left to the supervisor to determine as work proceeds. In view of the aesthetic factors involved, this is not always a sensible solution and supervisors should ensure that tolerance issues are raised with site management at the time site dimensions are taken and the work is set out.

KEEPING ADEQUATE RECORDS OF SETTING-OUT

It might, on occasions, be necessary for first line supervisors to keep a record of the setting-out procedures they have used. This may be particularly valuable where adjustments have had to be made to some of the work dimensions for a variety of reasons. Of course, keeping detailed records of every piece of setting-out is neither possible nor sensible, but there are often good reasons for doing so, including:

SETTING-OUT RECORDS – SOME REASONS WHY	• instances where dimensions have not been shown on drawings and have been agreed on site • occasions where errors or excessive tolerances have been found in the existing construction work, and it has been decided to adjust the new components to fit the existing work rather than make alterations to the existing work • where several different work teams are working in the same area and it is necessary to inform these other teams of the size and location of some aspect of the work • where it is necessary to make several similar components or where additional components may be needed at a later stage in the construction process • where those responsible for the management and maintenance of the building may require templates for replacement parts

- where there may be disagreements at a later stage regarding the sizes of the work and sources of the information on which setting-out decisions were made.

The general rule should be that if there are any doubts about the setting out or the dimensional accuracy of the work, then these should be recorded at the time the work is set-out, and proper instructions obtained regarding the appropriate action to be taken. Once this has happened these instructions and setting-out records should be kept for future reference because of increased costs or the appearance of latent defects.

SUMMARY

First line supervisors will normally have some responsibilities for setting-out, and for the equipment that will be required for this work. Also supervisors will often be responsible for checking the setting-out done by other people and for taking site dimensions to enable components to be manufactured away from the site.

It is important for supervisors to work from accurate instructions when planning setting-out and to work from established control points or temporary bench marks. Supervisors will need to consider what tolerances are appropriate for the work and how deviations in the sizes of components and in joint thicknesses can be accommodated during setting-out.

Finally, it should be remembered that occasionally supervisors will be well advised to keep records of the setting-out procedures they have used.

FURTHER STUDY OPPORTUNITIES

The following give further details regarding setting-out procedures on construction sites:

BRIGHTY, S. G., *Setting Out: a Guide for Site Engineers*, Granada 1981

BUILDING RESEARCH ESTABLISHMENT, *Accuracy in Setting-out*, BRE Digest 234, HMSO 1980

BS 5606, *Code of Practice for Accuracy in Building*, British Standards Institute 1978

MURPHY, R. W., *Site Engineering*, Construction Press 1983

RYAN, N. M., *Accuracy and Dimensional Control in Building*, Dublin, An Foras Forbatha 1980

SADGROVE, B. M., *Setting-out Procedures*, Butterworths 1988

CHAPTER THIRTEEN

WORKING IN OCCUPIED PREMISES

This chapter considers the special challenges which face the first line supervisor when work takes place in occupied buildings. A large, and growing, percentage of construction work now takes place in occupied buildings, and this work varies from simple maintenance tasks and the replacement of failed components to modernization schemes and alterations.

Almost always the occupants will consider the work to be of some inconvenience, often because buildings are seldom designed with maintenance in mind. Therefore it may be necessary for the supervisor to adopt different working methods in occupied buildings from those appropriate when working on new construction sites. It may also be necessary to balance the desire for good customer relations against the requirements of the contract.

Because the work may be located in someone else's place of work, bathroom or kitchen, shopping area or in a place of public entertainment, more attention may need to be given to the hazards associated with the work and the workplace, and once the work is finished the occupant may need some guidance regarding operating, cleaning and maintenance issues. Further consideration will now be given to some of these issues.

LIAISON WITH THE OCCUPANTS

Liaison is a process through which the contractor's representative and the occupants communicate during the process of the work. Effective liaison will usually require regular meetings and the first line supervisor will often have a crucial part to play in this process. In most occupied buildings there will be someone who has a special interest in the normal day to day activities associated with that building. This person may be a housewife or a shop or office manager with no particular knowledge or previous experience of building work, or it may be someone with both a detailed knowledge of the building and experience of the work to be done.

SETTING-UP PROCEDURES

Therefore, except perhaps in cases of emergencies, the liaison process begins with the first line supervisor making arrangements to visit the building some days or weeks before the work is due to start, in order to establish the exact nature of the work, and to explain the setting-up procedures for starting work on the project.

At the time of this initial visit by the first line supervisor, a formal contract between the client and the main contractor should be in existence. Where the first line supervisor is employed by a specialist contractor, there may also exist a sub-contract between the main contractor and the sub-contractor. This may involve the first line supervisor in additional negotiations, during which there are meetings between the first line supervisor and the main contractor's site representatives.

Following these meetings, it is usually essential for the first line supervisor to make direct contact with the occupants. However, the occupants of the building are not always the client for the contract, and the client may not have explained the work in any detail to the occupants. So the principal objective of this initial meeting is to ensure that the occupants understand the nature of the work, and are prepared for the arrival of the work team at the premises.

Where there is a client's representative, who is more or less resident in the building and who has a technical understanding of the work, the first line supervisor's task in explaining the nature of the work is simplified. In these situations this initial meeting will largely consist of the client's representative explaining the nature and location of the work to the first line supervisor. Consequently, it will usually be the responsibility of the client's representative to see that any occupants likely to be affected by the work are properly informed of the actions they should take when work is due to start. However, in many instances the occupants will have no real understanding of the nature of the work and will not have been informed of when the work is due to start or how long it might take. Therefore the first line supervisor will have to spend some time describing the work to the occupants. This can become a complex and time consuming exercise.

For example, a contract to rewire a block of 90 flats will involve separate discussions with the occupants of each flat, and the outcome of each of those discussions may have some influence on the sequence of operations, and on the preparatory work to be undertaken by the occupants, such as moving furniture and allowing access to the work at agreed times. This process can be even more difficult if the occupants do not have English as their first language, are elderly or disabled, or if the dwelling is overcrowded. Some contracts require the contractor to make special arrangements for tenant liaison, by appointing someone specifically for this task, and in such cases the first line supervisor has a less onerous task.

During this initial visit the first line supervisor should consider at least the following issues, although the exact nature of the work in each project will determine the specific issues to consider in each case:

THE INITIAL VISIT – SOME BASIC CONSIDERATIONS

- when the supervisor will require access to that part of the occupied building
- the length of time required to complete the work
- whether other work teams will have to complete their work before this operation can start, and whether there will be more work to follow on afterwards
- what the sequence of operations will be
- what dimensions need to be taken and what other preliminary tasks have to be completed by the first line supervisor before work can start
- what actions the occupants should take prior to work starting
- what decisions the occupants are required to make regarding the nature of the work, such as choice of colours and the position of fittings
- what the major inconveniences might be for the occupants, such as noise, smell, dust, length of time without main services, length of time when the occupants cannot use a particular area
- what precautions or protections the supervisor might need to consider in order to minimize inconvenience
- what other issues need to be resolved before work can start but which need to be raised with people other than the occupants.

Wherever possible at this first meeting a firm start date should be agreed. This may not always be possible because of the need for preliminary actions. This is why it is so necessary to hold this first meeting some time before work is due to start. Where firm start dates cannot be given the occupants must be informed later of the exact start dates.

During this first visit the supervisor will need to consider other issues such as:

SOME SETTING-UP ISSUES

- safe storage areas for materials and plant
- whether office and welfare facilities will be needed and if so where they should be located
- what detailed information will be needed before orders can be placed for plant and materials
- the potential hazards that exist and the precautions to be taken to guard against them.

REGULAR PROGRESS MEETINGS

Once work has started, there will also be a need for regular meetings between the supervisor, the occupants and the client's representative. The purpose of these meetings will be to review progress, to deal with problems as they arise and to keep the occupants informed of any changes that are necessary to the work, or to the sequence in which it is to be completed.

It may also be necessary to arrange regular times throughout the period of the work when occupants can meet the supervisor to discuss issues as they arise. It is sometimes appropriate to have a surgery hour when occupants can come to the supervisor's office for this purpose. Liaison can be a time consuming business and the first line supervisor must have some guidance of the amount of time that should be devoted to this process, and the amount of help that might be available from others in this respect.

ESTABLISHING SUITABLE WORKING PROCEDURES

Once the first line supervisor has a clear understanding of the terms and conditions of the contract, has visited the places where the work is to be done, and has established contact with the occupants it will be necessary to determine suitable working procedures. These procedures will be influenced by:

WORKING PROCEDURES – SOME BASIC ISSUES	<ul><li>the hours during which the work team will be allowed **access** to the building, or that part of the building where work has to take place</li><li>restrictions that have been imposed regarding **security, noise, dust**, etc</li><li>the **preparations** that are necessary before work can start</li><li>access to electricity for **power hand tools**</li><li>the need to **disconnect services** and the effect this will have upon the normal activities of the occupants, and the notice to be given before services may be disconnected</li><li>restrictions imposed upon the **unloading and movement of materials** for the work.</li></ul>

PROGRAMMES OF WORK

The outcome of these considerations should be the preparation of draft programmes of work or method statements in which the proposed sequence of operations is described in some detail. These programmes should then be discussed and agreed: first with the supervisor's senior management; secondly with any other associated work teams and finally, with the occupants and the client's representatives. Wherever possible, and this is usually only possible where the work is of a repetitive nature, an isolated section of the work should be completed as a pilot project. This will enable the work team to find out any problems associated with the work which are not apparent before work starts, and it will provide a guide to the time actually required to complete a section of the work. It will also provide a reference for the client regarding the sequence of the work, of the inconveniences which are likely to arise during its progress, and of the quality of the finished product. Thus it is important to involve the client's representative in all stages of the work to this pilot project.

LEARNING FROM EXPERIENCE OF THE WORK

With most repetitive work to occupied buildings both the occupants and the work teams learn from the experiences gained as the work proceeds. Therefore the first line supervisor should recognize that the early stages of the work will, to some extent, be exploratory and as a consequence performance should improve as the project proceeds.

This will only be true where the work is essentially similar throughout the project, where the composition of the work teams remains relatively stable, and where the client and the occupants do not make frequent changes to their requirements. Thus it is normal for the working procedures to change as the work progresses. This learning process requires very careful monitoring by the first line supervisor. Where work starts in unoccupied, or otherwise low priority areas, and standards are based on the experiences gained, problems may arise as the work proceeds to the more difficult or sensitive areas. Similarly, occupants may start out by being helpful but might become more demanding as they experience increasing inconvenience during the work. Therefore the learning process does not always result in a faster rate of completion for each section of the work. The time allowed for each section of the work should always include some provision for the uncertainties associated with work in occupied premises. It is unwise, even when trying to minimize the inconvenience to occupants, to programme for every task to be completed without some delay.

WORKING TO THE AGREED PROGRAMME

In order to have some chance of keeping to a programme of work, the first line supervisor should appreciate that:

WORK PROG-RAMMING – SOME BASIC ISSUES	• all programmes should be based upon a thorough analysis of the requirements of the contract, with no necessary element of work omitted • each stage of the work should be familiar to the work team and tested out in advance if there are any doubts regarding the nature or complexity of the work

- arrangements for the work should be agreed in advance with the occupants, so that they can make all the required preparations for the work to start at the agreed time and to proceed without delay
- some allowance should be made for problems that could not be foreseen.

Consequently, even with the most thorough programming, most tasks are likely to finish either slightly before, or slightly after, they were scheduled to finish. Where there are likely to be reasonably large overlaps or delays, the first line supervisor should ensure that everyone affected knows why this has happened, and what actions are being taken to bring the work back in line with the programme.

ALTERATIONS TO THE PROGRAMME OF WORK

There will be occasions when the client, or the occupants, want to alter the contract arrangements by introducing changes as the work proceeds, for which they will expect adjustments in the contract sum. There may also be occasions when the client, or the occupants, will impede the progress of the work by, for example, not allowing access to areas of the building as agreed, by not having areas cleared so that work can start on time, by requiring the work to be stopped or the sequence of the work to be changed, for reasons that were not appreciated at the time the programme was agreed.

DELAYS

When delays happen the first line supervisor should have some means of reporting back to the client and the occupants as well as to senior management, so that a revised programme can be prepared and agreed. It is not good practice to allow progress to deviate widely from the programme without some remedial actions being taken, otherwise occupants will be even more inconvenienced and the client will not appreciate that the work is delayed with cost implications to consider.

MINIMIZING HAZARDS

Working in occupied buildings presents potentially more hazards to health, safety and security than does work on a new construction site. This is because the occupants of the building may not appreciate the hazards that are associated with the work, and because there may be visitors to the premises who do not realize that construction activities are taking place. Therefore supervisors have to be even more careful about health, safety and security issues when working in occupied premises.

SAFETY ISSUES

With safety issues it may be necessary for the first line supervisor to consider:

SAFETY –
SOME BASIC
CONSIDERA-
TIONS

- the hazards associated with every stage of the work, with every material and item of plant to be used in each workplace
- the extent to which specialist help is required in order to assess the range of safety issues that might exist, particularly when specialized work is taking place in unfamiliar surroundings
- what precautions are necessary to guard operatives, occupants and visitors to the area from possible injury
- whether there are occupants and visitors who might need special care and attention in order to avoid injury, such as very young children, the elderly, blind, deaf or the physically or mentally disabled
- who is to be responsible for ensuring that these precautions are available and are used when work is in progress
- whether there are stages of the work where the hazards are so serious that occupants and visitors must be excluded from the workplace
- whether it is necessary for employees to have any special instruction or training in order to minimize the risks of injury to occupants and visitors
- whether it is necessary to inform occupants and visitors of the hazards associated with the work and, if so, how this is to be done
- whether it is necessary to inspect every workplace at the end of each work period in order to ensure that the area is free from any major safety hazards associated with the work.

HEALTH ISSUES

With health issues it may be necessary for the first line supervisor to consider:

HEALTH –
SOME BASIC
CONSIDERA-
TIONS

- whether any aspects of the work are likely to present particular hazards to health of the members of the team, occupants or visitors
- whether there are any occupants or visitors who are especially susceptible to particular health hazards, such as the elderly or those with heart or respiratory illnesses
- what precautions are necessary to protect operatives, occupants and visitors from any health hazards associated with the work

- who has the responsibility for assessing the risks, identifying the precautions to be taken and seeing that they are available and properly implemented
- whether any of the health risks are sufficiently severe to require occupants and visitors to be excluded from the area whilst work is in progress
- if exclusion from the work place is necessary, what refuge facilities are available for occupants
- what means might be used to determine when the area is free from health hazards so that occupants may return
- whether any special notification to occupants of the health risks is necessary and, if so, who is responsible for making such notifications.

SECURITY ISSUES

With security issues it may be necessary for the supervisor to consider:

SECURITY – SOME BASIC CONSIDERA- TIONS	<ul><li>what the contract conditions require regarding identity cards for employees</li><li>whether it is necessary to inspect each workplace before work starts in order to identify any security issues that require attention</li><li>whether special precautions are necessary, particularly regarding fire, flood, illegal entry and for the security of the occupants' property and operations</li><li>whether special security arrangements are necessary regarding the delivery and storage of plant and materials</li><li>whether regular security inspections are necessary as the work proceeds and if so, who should accompany the supervisor on such inspections</li><li>whether security inspections should be made at the end of each work period to ensure that each area in which work has taken place has been left in a secure condition</li><li>what procedures should be introduced for dealing with breaches of security when these have been identified.</li></ul>

First line supervisors need to be aware of the special security problems which might arise when working in particular types of buildings including: listed buildings, hospitals, and the homes of the elderly and disabled.

OPERATING AND MAINTENANCE ISSUES

Work in occupied buildings often results in the installation of equipment or components which occupants will need to:

- operate safely and effectively
- clean and maintain throughout the working life of the equipment.

Once new equipment has been installed and commissioned, occupants and operators will need to be trained in how to use it effectively. It is generally insufficient to leave the manufacturer's instructions lying around and hope someone will see them. With complex equipment and trained operators, the supervisor might need to consider:

FUTURE MAINTENANCE – SOME BASIC CONSIDERATIONS	• the need to pass over copies of the drawings or specifications of the installation and to trace the main features of the equipment with the operator • where as-built drawings and operating manuals are required, to ensure that these have been prepared and used as the basis of familiarization or training sessions with the operators • whether lists of spare parts or essential components are required • whether it is appropriate to label the controls and to provide checklists of the principal control setting operations • whether there is a need to pass on information about any after care servicing provided, including the names and telephone numbers of those to contact in the event of emergencies or problems arising during the defects liability period or period of warranty.

Where the equipment is to be operated by occupants with no special experience, it may be necessary for the supervisor to consider:

THE USERS – SOME BASIC CONSIDERATIONS	• what actions are necessary to ensure that the occupant knows the purpose of the equipment and its principal controls, and how and when these are to be operated or adjusted • what documentation should be left with the occupant • what actions the occupant should take if the equipment ceases to function properly and who to contact if specialist help is required • whether there are handbooks, registration documents, warranties or guarantees which have to be left with someone other than the occupant

- whether there are arrangements to be made for servicing with people other than the occupants.

It may also be necessary for the supervisor to give the occupant guidance on appropriate cleaning procedures, and any day to day maintenance which the occupant needs to undertake to ensure that the equipment remains in good working order. All first line supervisors should ensure that someone understands all the equipment controls, can diagnose the main malfunctions that are likely to occur and appreciates the maintenance and servicing requirements.

SUMMARY

Working in occupied premises raises additional issues for the first line supervisor. Foremost of these is the need for careful liaison with occupants in order to explain how the work will be sequenced and what precautions need to be taken to minimize inconvenience to the occupants. This liaison process will normally involve meetings and the preparation of programmes of work which may need to consider the effects of learning from the early experiences of the work.

Working in occupied premises also raises issues regarding alterations and customization of the work and the extent to which these can be accommodated within agreed programmes or will cause delays and increased costs. The additional health, safety and security issues associated with working in occupied premises will also need careful consideration. Finally, supervisors will need to ensure that occupants can operate, clean and maintain all new equipment safely and effectively.

FURTHER STUDY OPPORTUNITIES

The following give a more detailed appreciation of the issues involved in working in occupied buildings:

CIOB, *Maintenance Management – a Guide to Good Practice*, Chartered Institute of Building, 3rd edition 1989

CIOB, *Managing Building Maintenance*, Chartered Institute of Building nd

LEE, R., *Building Maintenance Management*, William Collins and Sons, 3rd edition 1987

CONCLUSIONS

The main activities of first line supervisors in the construction industry are addressed in this book, and the knowledge, skills and attitudes needed to perform the role effectively are described, also the challenging nature of the first line supervisor's job is demonstrated. A challenge which was expressed most elegantly by William van Dersal in *The Successful Supervisor* (Pitman 1970) as follows:

> There are few jobs more difficult but at the same time more interesting than that of supervising people. This takes more skill, more common sense, more imagination, more good humour, and certainly as much intelligence as any other kind of work. And it can frequently hold more grief, more trouble, and more difficulties than any other kinds of work, particularly for the man or woman who has not learned the art of working with other people.

In my career in the British construction industry I have found that first line supervision has been an area of considerable neglect, with only a very small percentage of practising craft supervisors in Britain having any supervisory training whatsoever. As a consequence most first line supervisors have developed their supervisory skills through experience. Some have been fortunate enough to work in organizations where training and guidance have been provided; others have been given no preparation for the challenges of the work and have developed working methods that have reflected their personal experiences.

This book provides insight into the main principles of first line supervision and thus enables individual supervisors to compare their own working methods, and the practices adopted within their employer's organizations with those suggested here. In some instances further, or deeper, study may be required and for this purpose references have been given at the end of each chapter.

Because of the crucial link first line supervisors provide between managers and operatives it is vital that employers give careful consideration to their supervisory training strategies and to the support they will need to give to inexperienced supervisors. Therefore managers and trainers can use this book to assist in the design of appropriate supervisory training programmes, and supporting manuals and procedures. The detailed day-to-day practices of craft supervision have not been considered, as these will be influenced by the nature of the work undertaken, and the structure and culture of the organizations in which first line supervisors are employed.

There is an obvious need in any large organization to review procedures regularly, not just those within each specialist department, but also those that require the positive actions of supervisors. Some guidance is therefore provided for those responsible for establishing procedures and for monitoring their effectiveness with first line supervisors.

INDEX